10-2-13

San Juan
River Chronicle

San Juan River Chronicle

Personal Remembrances of One of America's Best-known Trout Streams

Steven J. Meyers

WESTWINDS
PRESS®

Library of Congress Cataloging-in-Publication Data

Meyers, Steven J.
  San Juan River chronicle : personal remembrances of one of America's best-known trout streams / Steven J. Meyers.
    pages cm.
  Originally published: New York : Lyons & Burford, 1994.
    ISBN 978-0-87108-969-4 (paperback)
    ISBN 978-0-87108-984-7 (e-book)
    ISBN 978-0-87108-987-8 (hardbound)
  1. Trout fishing—San Juan River (Colo.-Utah) 2. Trout fishing—New Mexico.
3. San Juan River (Colo.-Utah)—Environmental conditions. 4. San Juan River (Colo.-Utah)—Description and travel. 5. Meyers, Steven J. 6. Fishers—San Juan River (Colo.-Utah)—Biography. I. Title.
  SH688.U6M49 2013
  799.17'57—dc23
                            2013021392

Interior Design by Jean Andrews
Cover Design by Vicki Knapton

Cover photo by Roger Hirst

WestWinds Press®
An imprint of

GRAPHIC ARTS
BOOKS®

P.O. Box 56118
Portland, OR 97238-6118
(503)254-5591
www.graphicartsbooks.com

To mentors and friends,
and to Bud Collins, who is both.

CONTENTS

ACKNOWLEDGMENTS

ODDLY, I FIND the task of committing an acknowledgment to paper even more daunting than that of writing a book, which is daunting enough. The number of people whose kindness, knowledge, and generosity have influenced the content of this book extends far beyond the few I have room to thank here, but to leave my gratitude unexpressed is unthinkable. I thank the many patient mentors who began the process of teaching me the ways of trout, and especially Jim Bell who is, sadly, gone. I would like to thank my colleagues on the river. The guides of the San Juan are an amazing lot, and they have generously shared both information and friendship—their contributions to this book have been enormous. I am especially indebted to John Flick and Tom Knopick of Duranglers, to Joe Kresl and Mike Crowley. I thank my clients, some of whom appear in these pages, for allowing me to see the river through their eyes.

I thank Roger Hirst for his good company on the river, and for the use of his lovely photograph for the cover of this book.

For his patient encouragement, and wise and thoughtful counsel, I can never thank Nick Lyons enough.

I owe more than I can ever express to my wife, Debbie, whose heart is larger than life, and whose perceptions broaden my own immeasurably. To my son, Daniel, I owe an equal debt. It is when I think of them that I feel most humbled and most inadequate in this attempt to express my gratitude.

Finally, I gratefully acknowledge the generosity of spirit of my great and wonderful friend Bud Collins. I cannot begin to list all that he has contributed to this book.

Read on, and you'll know why I find it easier to write books than acknowledgments. You'll also discover why this one never would have been possible without Bud.

INTRODUCTION

THIS MORNING, walking from the house to my study in the wet-snow squall of a mid-February storm, I found myself musing on the truthfulness of clichés, dreaded clichés, those truisms to be avoided in print at all cost.

Like most writers, I find myself stringing sentences together at the oddest moments. Those moments often have nothing to do with sitting in front of a computer, fingers poised over a keyboard. Sometimes, if I'm watching and not fishing when a trout dimples the surface of a lake so calm it has become a mirror and the mountains and sunset sky above it are reflected so perfectly it is hard to tell which are the mountain and sky, which the lake, I'll find myself thinking . . . *a lake so calm it had become a mirror and the mountains and sunset sky above it reflected so perfectly it was hard to tell which were the mountain and sky and which the lake.* This is hardly the way to be present in the world. This is not a statement of pride; it is a confession. Sometimes the writer in me is more in his head than in this world. But not too often and almost never when I'm actually fishing. Perhaps that is one reason why I love fishing so much.

This morning, walking between my warm bed and my sure to be frigid studio (I would have to turn on the electric heater to take off the chill), the

11

smell of snow struck me suddenly. Like a hammer. Like a snowflake. I was immediately transported to the San Juan, to The Split, and to a similar morning twenty-five years ago.

The river could be crowded, even then, on summer weekends. The paths to the most popular spots were there, but they were far less deeply worn than they are now. A few places in the quality water—the first few miles of river below Navajo Dam and upstream from the RVs and tents at Cottonwood Campground—still had no path at all, nothing worn through the willows that screamed, "Fish here!" At that time, The Split was still something of a secret. And in the winter, in the middle of a storm? It was almost certain to be devoid of anglers but full of trout rising to midges.

Twenty-five years ago, on a morning similar to the snowy one that is visible now outside my window, Bud Collins and I drove down to the river sliding around slick curves, spinning wheels on the steeper hills as we slowly worked our way south. When we opened the doors of my Jeep to get out and pull on our waders it was there, the smell of snow.

This morning, when the memory struck, I found myself writing in my head the dreaded cliché:

No sense is as evocative of memory as the sense of smell.

But dammit, it's true, and this morning when the smell of snow filled my nostrils I was immediately transported back to the San Juan, The Split, the company of one of the best fishing buddies I ever had and the presence of large gray trout sipping the tiniest of gray flies in a gray river beneath a gray sky opposite tall, gray sandstone cliffs obscured by snowflakes the size and shape of mallard breast feathers that landed in the stillness with a discernible *plop*.

Another gray day, one much like that one is described in this book.

~

This is the introduction to a new edition of a book about the San Juan River that I wrote nearly twenty years ago. At the time I first wrote the book, I had been fishing the river for almost the same amount of time that has now passed since the book's initial appearance. Between the morning I first set foot in the San Juan River and the first writing of this book a lot of changes had taken place. A river that had been relatively unknown had been discovered. A river that once saw crowds only in its uppermost stretches, close to the dam, a river that fished exceptionally well for many miles but was left virtually untouched in its lower reaches had been explored, mapped, and guide-booked—places Bud and I once fished alone only after parking our car on the shoulder of the deserted road and bushwhacking through dense willow were now often filled with anglers who walked a well-worn trail to the river after parking in one of the newly paved lots that dotted the landscape.

Another twenty years have passed and the river has seen more change. In the early 1990s there was a growth in fly fishing unlike any the sport had previously seen. The boom roughly coincided with the release in 1992 of Robert Redford's film version of Norman Maclean's wonderful novella, *A River Runs Through It,* and many consider that movie to have been the catalyst. I'm not so sure. I had seen fly fishing—the only fishing for trout I knew about for much of my childhood, shielded as I'd been from other kinds of fishing by a wise and capable hunting and fishing father—gradually grow in popularity throughout my life. Before Brad Pitt ever appeared onscreen in suspenders and fedora wielding a fly rod, the popularity of fly fishing had begun to grow. Places where fly fishing was particularly good, places like the San Juan River, felt a degree of pressure that threatened to destroy them.

I alluded to that growth in the first edition of this book, but I was also able to describe an experience of the river that was not dominated by crowds—a river of quiet joy and solitude, a river where the profound and hard-earned pleasures of extremely technical fishing could be learned and where deep friendships flourished. That river, I am very happy to report, still exists.

~

Rivers, like individuals, like economies, like nations go through periods of plenty and periods of privation. Rivers have cycles. Some are measured in minutes. A cloud obscuring the sun might bring trout to the surface to feed.

The passing of that cloud, the reappearance of the sun, will often drive trout back to the bottom. Other cycles are measured in hours, days, weeks, months, years, and decades. Some, beyond our experiencing, stretch out over millennia.

In the time I have been fishing it, the San Juan below Navajo Dam has experienced decadeslong periods when water was plentiful and one decade of severe drought that radically altered the nature of the fishing.

Summer thunderstorms wash many tons of silt into long stretches of the river whose cold, oxygenated water and clean cobbles are the perfect habitat for massive populations of aquatic life—including mayflies, stone flies, and caddis. Silt accumulates as a result of sudden summer floods in the sandy side canyons and arroyos that enter the river below the dam. When that silt is not flushed out by large spring releases it remains in the river covering the cobbles. Vegetation takes root in it, and the trout food in a river once the home to a wide variety of aquatic insects becomes less varied, other trout foods more at home in the changed environment become more prominent.

In one ten-year period between the writing of the first edition of this book and this new edition such a change took place. During those drought years, silt accumulated throughout the river. Riverbed habitat became more and more suited to a smaller variety of aquatic insect life and to other aquatic invertebrates. Many who didn't know the river better would have told you that the river was best fished, always, with some kind of annelid (most likely red)—a fly pattern named after a phylum of segmented worms that mimics any number of larva and worm-like invertebrates that flourish in silted river bottoms—and a midge pupa. One of the great dry fly rivers of the West had become, for many fishermen, a place only to nymph. A river once known for prolific mayfly hatches throughout much of the year, for sudden and surprising stone-fly hatches and reliable caddis hatches in the late summer became, to many, an "annelid" and midge river.

Which is not to say the other bugs had gone away. They were simply not quite as prevalent as they had once been. They were biding their time.

In the time between editions of this book, the New Mexico Department of Game and Fish has worked diligently to restore and preserve the extraordinary fishery that is the San Juan River below Navajo Dam. Rock structures were installed in the lower stretches of the river to provide deeper pools for trout during times of low water. These structures provided depth, but they also created scouring currents that cleaned cobbles of silt and restored some of the varied river-bottom habitat that again produces prolific mayfly hatches. In The Braids, a great deal of work has likewise been done to deepen pre-existing channels and create scouring currents. Where a side canyon particularly prone to flooding and the introduction of silt enters the river, a settling pond has been built. This has reduced the negative impact of summer storms. Cobbles are reappearing in places where they hadn't been seen in years. More varied insect life is returning.

~

This past spring, I spent a day on the river with a dear friend from Greeley in northern Colorado. Jim had come down to fish for the weekend and it was clear to both of us without either of us having to say a word that The Juan would be on our itinerary. The day we spent on the river was a warm day in May with alternating cloud and sun. Maybe because it was a place we had fished together so many times before, maybe because it was a place that a years-on-the-river hunch told us would fish well that day, we headed for Baetis Bend. We arrived on the water around 10:00 in the morning. Trout were up on midges so we rigged with dry flies. Jim chose a spot near the bottom of the bend, walking out on a spit of sand below the island that divides the river between Baetis Bend proper and the Baetis Bend back channel. I wandered upriver a bit, pausing to cast whenever I saw a trout rising. The trout ate midges for a few hours until mayfly duns began appearing. For a while a trout might take either, but eventually the fish settled into the rhythmic sipping of duns. I switched from a tiny parachute Adams to an Olive Sparkle Dun and kept finding trout willing to eat my dry fly.

Jim, visible downstream, always seemed to have a trout splashing at the end of his leader.

A few boats passed by. Several were rowed by guide friends who yelled out a friendly greeting as they passed at a distance—graciously avoiding a close pass that would put down the fish I was working. No wading fishermen, other than Jim, were visible to me. I guessed the few cars we'd seen in the lot belonged to anglers who had hiked upstream to the Lower Flats. Around 2:00 in the afternoon, the hatch dwindled. I reeled in my line and walked down to gather up Jim for a sandwich and a break. For four hours we'd had the river and rising trout pretty much to ourselves.

This past fall, another good friend, Jon, came to visit. On that September day the sun was hiding. An occasional shower peppered us, but mostly it was cloudy without rain. On that day the little voice in my head had whispered, *The Split, fish The Split.* Jon agreed, so that's where we headed. We emerged from the willows to see one boat anchored near the head of The Split some fifty yards out in the river. Jon and I separated. He headed upriver and I walked down to where a large back channel parted from the main current. It took me a few minutes to see them, but once my eyes began to adjust to the light and what was going on in the water trout were as plain beneath the surface as they might have been if they'd been taking flies on top. There, in the still pool just above the place where the back channel dove into a riffle, dozens of trout were suspended in mid-depth eating. I could see their mouths opening and closing quickly, see the flash of white that created, see the occasional wiggle of a tail or turn of a head that allowed a trout to move the inch or less it required to grab food as it drifted by. I rigged with a midge emerger, placing the tiniest piece shot I had above the tippet knot. I greased my leader down to about three feet above the shot and began to cast.

The sky remained cloudy. Rain fell lightly every now and then. After a little while the guide in the now distant boat raised anchor, waved a silent good-bye, and moved off downriver with his client. I looked upriver to see Jon hunched over in keen concentration. Once in a while, I looked and saw him playing a trout. Every now and then one of the fish feeding in front of me would move that sudden inch or open its mouth revealing that telltale flash of white as my fly was entering its mouth; I would strike downstream, quickly, and feel the line tighten as I securely embedded my fly in the corner of the trout's mouth.

On that damp morning in the fall of 2012, long after many had written off the San Juan River as a far too crowded place, Jon and I fished alone, surrounded by feeding trout. Large trout. Clean trout without a mark. Difficult, picky trout that would only eat an artificial fly that was very much like the naturals in the river. Subtle trout that ate so softly you would not catch them if you waited for a strike indicator to move. You hooked them only by seeing them take your artificial fly. We had these magnificent fish all to ourselves.

~

Changes have taken place on the river. You can no longer fish the water within a few hundred yards of the dam. Homeland security and the aftershock of 9/11 have rendered that water off-limits. Brown trout have gradually come to occupy the upper reaches of the quality water. When I first wrote the book, rainbows dominated and brown trout were quite rare. Now, brown trout are common, and I believe they have made the experience of fishing the San Juan even more wonderful. River improvements have created better, new and different fishing in some places. But the most important, the most wonderful things have not changed since I first discovered this amazing fishery or since this book was first released. The San Juan River below Navajo Dam is still one of the most extraordinary trout fisheries in the American West. It is still a place where strong, healthy trout live in the near ideal conditions created by regulated, cold-water releases from a large impoundment. It is still one of the best places in the world to learn the ways of selective trout and how to fish tiny flies on fine tippets. It is still a place where trout, angling skills, and friendships all grow. It is still a river where a person seeking solitude and profound pleasure can find them.

Steven J. Meyers
Durango, February 9, 2013

PREFACE

Could we know what men are most apt to remember,
we might know what they are most apt to do.

—George Savile

IT WAS A QUANDARY, and not one I could resolve easily. I have written in the past about the joys of fly fishing and the pleasures of the stream. I have tried to communicate the uniqueness of place and of my place in particular: the San Juan Mountains of southwestern Colorado. I have extolled the virtues of the small stream, and I have avoided—in my writing, at least—the esoteric technical minutiae of the sport. My approach has been simple: paint the angling with broad strokes; sketch the place, people, feelings, thoughts, and images in finer detail.

Shortly after I completed just such a book, my friend and editor, Nick Lyons, suggested that I think about doing a book on the San Juan River. I wondered why. Had I not recently written that such places could never be home water to me? Wasn't it clear that I considered my home to be the mountains and not the desert? But Nick is a friend and, what's more, he has proven to be a wise and perceptive friend. So, rather than dismiss the idea out of hand, I struggled with it. I wondered why Nick might have thought to ask me to consider such a book.

I began writing to Nick almost as soon as we became acquainted. The contents of that correspondence, often littered with thoughts and questions about my own writing and the writing of others, usually carried a fishing tale or two. I wrote to him about fishing because it was important to me. I did it because we write to our friends not only to share ideas, but to share experiences. I did it because I knew that fishing was something we both approached with great passion. I wrote to him about fishing because I know, as committed as he is to this delightful insanity, he is more committed to his family, his work, and a life that requires him to spend most of his time in a gray, hard city, away from the streams of the West he has come to love so much in recent years.

Nick wrote back to me from New York, and sometimes from a river—his favorite spring creek, or the banks of the Madison.

I realized after many such epistles, after his suggestion that I think about doing a book on the San Juan River, that many of the things I shared with Nick in my letters were experienced on the San Juan.

The San Juan River is a tailwater, a year-round fishery, and for much of the year it is the only place I can wet a fly; still, even after the snow has gone and the ice has melted from other streams, it remains a river of great challenge and pleasure—a place to work, a place to play. I wrote to Nick about solitude and beauty, about friendship, and of course, about the fishing. It was only natural for Nick to ask me to consider such a book.

But do we need another book about a well-known and hard-fished river? I'm not sure. As anyone who has fished the San Juan on a busy weekend will tell you, the crowds can be atrocious. I have experienced such crowds any number of places. I remember a day on Silver Creek during the Trico hatch when anglers arrived hours before the spinners began to fall in order to ensure that there would be a place for them in the water, a day when there was no place for me, a day when I had to wait until after the hatch to get into this beautiful spring creek to scrounge leftovers from beneath the undercuts and among the weeds with a nymph. I remember days on the Bighorn when guides nearly came to blows over other guides' boats being beached too close to their clients. I remember watching dory after dory on that famous river pass through the same rapid, fisherman after fisherman throwing flies behind the same boulder, boat after boat. And I wondered, "How much of this can these poor fish take?"

But this is not the kind of fishing I want to remember. The San Juan I choose to remember, the place I share with Nick in my letters, the river I write about now, is one of quiet back channels and spooky behemoths, of tiny dry flies stolen from the surface, of nymphs and pupae ambushed in the film. It is a river of remembrance, not of regret. It is a river that exists, fortunately, not only in the golden light of memory, but also in the quite real, extraordinarily lovely sunshine of the New Mexico desert; a river that winds through sandstone walls, rabbitbrush, and sage; a river that is found a short hike away from the parking lots, the easily accessible water, and the crowds.

QUALITY WATER

MY HOME RESTS on the border between two worlds—two worlds as different as ice and fire—that are connected to each other by clear running water and by trout. In the west, north, and east, mountains rise above the foothills that block my view of them. Although I cannot see the high mountains from my house beside the Animas River, I can feel them. A short hike into the nearby hills reveals their presence. The LaPlata Mountains rise over 13,000 feet a few short miles to the west. The big peaks of the high San Juans, snowcapped summits above 14,000 feet, rise twenty-five miles to the north. From a mountaintop perch in the center of this alpine world, a sea of stone and snow swells to the horizon in every direction—hundreds of towering peaks rise from the valleys and gorges of the countless rivers and creeks.

In the south there is sandstone and mesa—the stark rock walls and sparse growth of the desert. A journey south takes you into the desert, into the lush green tangle of piñon and juniper that covers the higher ground, the scattered grasses and deep sand of the low places and arroyos, into a desert that runs for hundreds of miles with little interruption from here to the Sonora. In the north, conifer and tundra predominate. In the south, chamisa and sage prevail.

Connecting these two worlds are the rivers that flow from the volcanic high San Juans into the desert: the San Juan, Piedra, and Pine; the Florida, Animas, and Dolores. Each of them has taught me about the ways of trout, but none has taught me better than the San Juan.

~

I came to the mountains shortly after graduate school in Chicago—not quite twenty years ago—and immediately set about catching mountain trout on the fly under the tutelage of a few wise old trout men, men who dabbled with the dry fly but reserved their deepest affection for soft-feathered beauties with names like Parmachene Belle and Pink Lady. From them I learned to swim a fly under light tension past the nose of a holding trout, to sense where the invisible artificial was swimming and how it behaved. I learned to strike on the subtle feel of a gentle take, on the flash of a fish's belly, or the wink of an open mouth. I often fished alone, with great intensity, honing the skills they taught me—stealth, reading the water, fly presentation, and control of the fly line.

~

Trout books became as much a passion as fishing itself, and through them I discovered that fly fishing had come a long way since the days of Parmachene Belle.

Books that dwell on technique have never been my favorites, but I could get wonderfully lost in books about place, in tales of human foibles that masqueraded as simple fishing stories, and although there was little of technique in my favorite books, I learned a great deal from writers like Roderick Haig-Brown and Robert Traver.

When I did turn to more technical writing, I found the best to be full of fishing, not formulas. I never would have learned to fish without Ray Bergman. He stood beside me at every pool, and I can remember wondering each time I entered a stream, "How would Ray fish this water?" I eagerly sought his advice and approval, recalling his descriptions of foolish anglers who spooked every trout on their first cast and wise fishermen who began with a short line and worked out toward distant water. I remembered his stories of fishermen who failed to strike wet flies that had found the mouths of willing trout only to be spat out, undetected, because the strike, when it finally came, came too late. I fished in the very long shadows of Sid Gordon, Vincent Marinaro, and Charles Fox. Joseph Bates guided my bucktails and streamers past the boulders and into the mouths of trout.

I learned to tie a respectable dry fly (tying dozens in a vise that a good friend, Jim Bell, had made for his daughter, Sandy, from a piece of bent steel rod—a vise she gave me when Jim passed away) and to fish it bobbing merrily without drag, upstream. I learned the difference between an attractor and an imitator, and I discovered the nymph. With each book, each lesson from my mentors, each day spent on the mountain streams of the San Juans I learned much, and found a great deal of pleasure.

~

Much has been written about the joys of fly fishing and about the progress of an individual as he learns the sport. It seems that the beginner almost always revels in numbers, and mountain streams are a good place to get this wonderful silliness out of your system. A competent angler on a fish-filled mountain stream can catch numbers of trout beyond belief. During the long, hot days of August, days after the runoff and before the early chill of autumn, a properly floated Elk Hair Caddis or Royal Trude will raise trout beyond counting. Soon the serious fisherman realizes that there is more to fishing than catching a lot of fish.

With enough time on the stream and perhaps a little expert tutelage, a fisherman discovers some truly fine fish, bigger fish, fish that pull hard enough to strip line from the reel and get the adrenaline flowing. He learns that these trout are not as plentiful as easier, smaller trout—it takes a bit more knowledge, a bit more skill and patience to catch them. Soon these are the fish that cause him to dream, the fish he tries to catch when he goes fishing.

Numbers go down, but rewards climb significantly. A fourteen-inch creek trout risen from a tiny slack-water eddy behind a rock, the trout that is protected beneath an overhanging tangle of branches, the trout that takes a fly in the single heart-stopping second of dead drift before hopeless drag sets in, the trout that leaps, crashing and tumbling downstream, is remembered for years—perhaps forever.

Which is not to say that experienced fishermen don't go back to easy fish now and then, to feel them tug, to admire their beauty, to know that the stream is alive and well. But a steady diet of easy fish quickly dulls the angler's pleasure.

And that's how it is with rivers.

~

When I speak of home water, I do so with reverence. Nothing is as close to my heart as the highland stream I call home. I love the mountains and the spruce forest. I feel more alive above 10,000 feet than anywhere else. My home water runs through alpine forest, beneath high mountains, and although it has taught me a lot, I know I have not learned everything it can teach me; yet, there are many things it can never teach me.

It cannot teach me about selective trout because the water is acidic, the environment harsh, and insects never appear in sufficient numbers to require such behavior of its trout. The trout who do best in the food-scarce water are the ones that seize food most aggressively. It cannot give me the experience of massive hatches and the wonderful rhythm of prevalent insects changing with the seasons. It cannot teach me the subtleties of difficult fly tying because the trout don't much care how well a fly is tied—if an artificial fly looks remotely like food and goes by without too much commotion (sometimes a little commotion is good), the fish eat it. It cannot show me the sophistication of trout who have been fished over and are—if not as spooky and wary of anglers as Lime Creek trout—infinitely more wary of the things they cast upon the water.

~

Many themes recur in the trout books I love. I particularly enjoy the rich literature of place that angling has inspired—books in which the rhythms of nature and the seasons are present, books in which the unique setting and character of a particular river are as much a personality in the narrative as any angler. Writing that recognizes, celebrates, and thoughtfully describes this aspect of fishing is my favorite writing. But there are other themes I enjoy as well. I enjoy the tales of friendship and adventure that flow readily from days on the trout stream. I love to read and marvel at the steady growth of knowledge and the development of angling technique.

One of the striking characteristics of fishing insight is the frequency with which it has come from people who have spent time unraveling the secrets of a single extraordinary river. Great anglers and great rivers are a wonderful combination. I think of Frank Sawyer developing his nymphs on the Avon, of Vincent Marinaro and Charles Fox exploring the secrets of terrestrials on the Letort. I picture big Jim Leisenring and Vernon Hidy lifting wet flies on the Brodheads, and Art Flick collecting insects on the Schoharie. Steelheading would not be what it is today without Fred Burnham and the lessons he learned and then graciously shared along the banks of the Umpqua.

On these and other rivers, those of us with less skill make our own discoveries. We learn our own lessons, and we learn them best when we take the time to know a place well.

~

For me, serious learning began with the high mountain streams, with the wet fly, and with mentors who rooted me firmly in the traditions of trout fishing. But the urge to push technique, to try new things, to catch difficult trout drew me inevitably to other rivers. I have sought trout in the tumbling freestone rivers of the Rocky Mountain West, in the limestoners of the East, and in the coastal rivers of British Columbia; but the opportunity to fish a single river throughout the year, learning some of the intricacies of trout that feed selectively on profuse hatches, the chance to fish day after day as the seasons and insects change, the occasion to tackle the puzzle of a single, difficult stream, was given to me by the San Juan River in northern New Mexico.

I marvel at the great good fortune that found me fishing in the company of wise, generous teachers. I am grateful for the knowledge I have gained from the literature of trout. But, in the end, I realize that there is one mentor that stands above all of those with whom I have fished, all of the books I have read, and that mentor is the river itself.

~

The San Juan River begins in the high mountains of the Weminuche Wilderness, in the eastern San Juans near the Continental Divide at Wolf Creek Pass. These mountains are the birthplace of many rivers. The headwaters of the Rio Grande tumble from their eastern flank. The upper Colorado River finds its flow greatly enhanced by streams that originate in the western and northern parts of the range—the San Juan River carries the flows of the Piedra, Pine, Florida, and Animas into the Colorado River at Glen Canyon (now buried beneath Lake Powell); the Dolores River follows a convoluted path from the western San Juans, southward, northward, and finally westward to the Colorado River in Utah, near Cisco; the Gunnison River joins the Colorado at Grand Junction in western Colorado after its flows have been broadened by branches, including the legendary Lake Fork, that flow from the northern San Juans.

In its upper reaches the San Juan River, like others that descend from the high mountains, was always trout water—cutthroat water. But as it lost elevation and flowed through Pagosa Springs, then past Arboles and into the sandstone canyons of New Mexico, it slowed, warmed, gathered silt, and lost its ability to sustain trout. From here to the Colorado River it was the home of pikeminnow, suckers, and chub.

All of that changed in 1962, with the completion of a high earthen dam in the narrow canyon of the San Juan just downstream from its confluence with the Pine River.

Anglers everywhere are familiar with the effects of cold water releases from the lakes that are impounded behind high dams. Throughout the country there are cold water fisheries in rivers that sustained only warm water species prior to the existence of these dams. The newly created fisheries are called "tailwaters," and the San Juan River below Navajo Dam is a prime example.

Water released from deep in the lake remains cold, with relatively constant temperature throughout the year. Silt that is carried from the mountains during runoff settles into the lake bottom. A river that once turned brown during snowmelt or heavy rain now runs clear below the dam. Flows that fluctuated wildly have been tamed, allowing more varied vegetation and invertebrate life to establish themselves. A river that once was home only to warm water species has become prime trout water.

Rainbow trout stocked in the San Juan following completion of the dam grew at an astonishing rate. Initial growth was in the neighborhood of six inches a year. Encouraged by the success of its early plantings of rainbows, the New Mexico Department of Game and Fish soon added brown trout (in 1964) and finally Snake River cutthroat (in 1978). The rainbows occasionally hybridize with the cutthroat, and sometimes an angler will find orange slashes on the throat of a fish that appears to be mostly rainbow trout. All three species, and the rainbow-cutthroat hybrids, have done well in the river, but none quite so well as the rainbow. It outnumbers the other trout by a wide margin, especially in the quality water that exists in the three and a half miles of river immediately below the dam.

The typical fish taken on the San Juan today is a deep-bodied, heavy rainbow trout of seventeen or eighteen inches that weighs around two pounds. And, as in many other of the well-known tailwaters of the West, it is possible to take trout far in excess of twenty inches—trout in the five- to eight-pound range. The number of fish in this class is astonishing; and, rather than being an extraordinary event, trout in excess of twenty inches are common. Trout of six and seven pounds are caught regularly.

What makes the catching of these heavy, hard-running fish even more extraordinary is the fact that much of the fishing is done during hatches of extremely small flies. Mayflies on this river are typically a size #20 or #22, and the predominant food, by far, is the midge, a two-winged aquatic insect that appears, most often, in a size #24 or smaller.

With the completion of the dam, the stocking of trout, and the passage of time, the San Juan River below Navajo Dam has become one of the world's premier large-trout, small-fly fisheries.

The fishing, however, is not limited to midges and tiny mayflies. Caddis appear on summer evenings, and stone flies occur, perhaps not as frequently as on nearby freestone water but often enough to provide some excellent fishing. Terrestrial fishing with crickets, hoppers, beetles, and ants can be extraordinary in the grass-lined back channels. A carpenter ant fall will bring every good fish in the river to the surface for a meal.

Like most trout water, the San Juan is a place where the fish feed predominantly beneath the surface. Good nymph fishermen do well here, and there are nymph opportunities on this river that are unlike those presented elsewhere. Many contemporary fishermen consider the nymph something of a lesser artificial. As it is often fished—tied to the end of a long, weighted leader, a bright strike indicator dancing on the surface, probing dark runs for unseen trout—nymph fishing is a very different sport from dry-fly fishing to rising trout. But many of the trout that feed beneath the surface of the transparent water of the San Juan do so in a foot or two of slow, clear water. They are visible fish, visibly feeding, sometimes easily spooked (sometimes not), but every bit as difficult as the dry-fly fish we try to catch. Sight nymphing with tiny flies to five-pound rainbows in shallow water is one of the great experiences in the sport of trouting, and the San Juan provides a lot of it.

There are other attributes of the fishery, attributes that make it a wonderful and challenging place to fish: profuse hatches, extreme selectivity, tricky currents, and difficult drifts.

It is, in short, a good place for an angler who has learned a great deal about easy trout to go to find something else. A great place, in fact, for me to go twelve years ago when I began fishing the river. I typically spend seventy or eighty days a year guiding the river, fishing the river, probing the

San Juan for trout and knowledge. It is the place I am most likely to find myself standing knee deep in cold water, pouring over a fly box, wondering what to do next.

~

I continue to spend a great deal of time on the mountain streams, casting a 7½-foot cane rod, swimming a Dark Cahill or drifting a Royal Trude, thinking about the men, now gone, who taught me to fish. There is no place that feels more like home to me than the half-mile stretch of Lime Creek, up in the mountains, that I fish regularly. I have learned the profound joy of a good friend's home water—Bud Collins's beloved Florida River. The deep gorge that is the Black Canyon of the Gunnison is filled with powerful trout that I have hooked, landed, or lost; they continue to run through the rapids of my dreams. I would take a day on the Campbell, the Quinsam, or the Stamp anytime I could get it, because I always feel that I am fishing in Haig-Brown's shadow when I am there, and it is a feeling that I love. I want to learn the intricacies of the Sol Due and the Hoh. I long to experience the wildness and mystery of the Olympic Peninsula.

Anadromous fish pull hard on me even when I am thousands of miles from coastal rivers. There are cold white winter weeks when I tie nothing but steelhead flies—dreaming of a precious few days in late summer or fall when I hope to sneak away for sea-runs. Someday, when I am too old to guide, when my eyesight grows poor and I have become the one who needs to borrow a younger man's eyes to tie on a midge, I hope to be able to spend months at a time getting to know new water—perhaps a spring creek in Idaho or Montana. But for now, when I think of rivers and trout, I always come back to the one that has been my most demanding yet generous teacher: the San Juan.

THE GRAY SEASON

I'VE OFTEN HEARD IT SAID that a river without friends is an endangered river—but there is a part of me that misses the time, not too many years back, when the San Juan had a few less friends. The winter used to belong to a handful of regulars. There once was a time when you could drive to the river on a warm winter day—a day of blue sky and hot sun, a day of hatching midges that clumped into fist-sized rafts in the eddies and drew gulping rises from trout; a day of Blue-Winged Olives that emerged from nymphal shucks in the flats, of huge fish that sipped the duns calmly in the clear, shallow water of Baetis Bend. Your face would feel the warmth of the sun and even if the temperature were in the thirties or lower forties, it would seem much warmer because of the thin air and the intense solar radiation. If you were able to get away on such a day, you almost always had great fishing, and you could always find a piece of river to yourself, a place to fish where you could look upriver and down without seeing another angler.

It's not like that anymore. Warm winter days bring out nearly as many fishermen as summer weekends, and the winter river is no longer a private place—except for the gray days.

There are few rules in fishing that hold—very few. Almost as soon as a rule is spoken, it is contradicted. Most fishermen believe that fishing stinks during the full moon (in my experience it often does), but every now and then I've had exceptional days on a full moon. Some people refuse to fish when a front is moving through. I've read that fish are off their feed when the barometer is changing because their swim bladders need time to adjust to changes in air pressure before they can find a comfortable equilibrium in the water. It is said that during this process they do not eat, but some of my very best fishing experiences have occurred with the coming of major storms and a dramatic drop in the barometer. There are rules regarding water clarity, rising and falling water levels, and the height of the sun, but none is inviolate. One rule, however, seems to hold more often than not, and I have let it be my guide for winter fishing: if you are willing to fish in bad weather, you can almost always have a piece of river to yourself. And you can often find good fishing.

Fishing binges are strange, and the reasons for them mysterious. They have the same logic—or lack of it—as cravings during pregnancy, the love of Fords or Chevys, white or black hats. There have been months when I would not fish a river, entire seasons when I fished only high-altitude lakes. I have spent years fishing small streams, years when the trout of big rivers were of absolutely no interest to me. I have lost weeks trying to catch a particular fish—a fish spotted while paddling a canoe or randomly fishing a river for other trout, a monster that appeared unexpectedly, its dark shadow moving slowly and deliberately from a lie previously unknown and unsuspected, a vision awakened by paddle or fly line. I have wasted months of my life trying to find those fish again . . . and, as often as not, I have failed.

Writing this, I remember a few fish that I never saw a second time, trout whose vague form lingers in memory, trout I want to seek one more time, even now, even though it has been years since I last saw any of them and it is likely none of them remain. There was a thirty-plus-inch submarine that moved slowly and deliberately from an undercut bank on one of the many forks of the South Platte River in Colorado's South Park. A trout that revealed itself when I stuck one of his smaller brethren—an eighteen-inch brown trout—with a streamer that had swung beneath that same undercut. Nearly twice the length of the fish I had hooked, it moved away slowly as the smaller trout struggled at the end of my leader. I am haunted by a vision that took all of my line and backing, racing downstream with the current, my heavy hand and stout 2X tippet no match for his strength or that of the raging currents of the Gunnison River. There are monsters in the Animas River as it flows through Durango—including one that vaulted above a rapid and landed with a racket more like that of a log being tossed into the water than the sound of a jumping fish, a trout that showed itself as I was casting to others that were taking dry flies in a nearby eddy. I am haunted by a great trout lost in the broad water of Simon Canyon on the San Juan. The trout feasted on nymphs in the tailout of a deep pool, inches above a glassy drop, just upstream from the powerful, churning white water of Simon Rapid. It took a flashback nymph and proceeded to drag me a quarter mile downriver as I ran along the bank, struggling to keep up. In the footrace that ensued I was hopelessly outclassed—a schoolboy up against an elite sprinter. The inevitable defeat came when the backing ran out and the leader snapped. I searched in vain for that trout for many months, hoping to hook him one more time, not having the slightest idea what I would do if I succeeded.

There was the winter binge, the year I fished every time it snowed, every time the radio warned, "The roads are bad—don't go out unless you absolutely have to!" It was a winter that found me merrily rolling through axle-deep snow, sliding through corners, barely able to keep the car moving as I pushed my way past Ignacio and the reservation, through the gas and oil fields, on over the dam (some might say over the edge) to the river.

Such lunacy experienced in isolation is the stuff of madness, but when it is shared with a friend it becomes something else: a noble passion, an enterprise, a quest. That winter Bud and I were equally obsessed and it would have been hard to say which of us played Sancho to the other's Quixote. We drove to the river on roads that had been abandoned by other travelers and even by the plows. The windshield wipers struggled to push wet, heavy snow from the glass. The car heater roared, and above it the buzz-saw strains of Joe Satriani's guitar alternated with more lyrical moments. Nancy Griffith sang of love won and lost in the scorching heat of west Texas. Lyle Lovett mixed his large band with acoustic guitar and wry humor.

That winter, we fished. We fished regularly. We fished in so much clothing that we could scarcely move. We fished, wringing wet with melted snow and perspiration—sweating beneath the layers when we hiked from one spot to the next, shivering with damp chill when we stopped to cast. We fished with numb fingers and raw, weather-beaten faces. I don't think I've ever enjoyed a winter more.

It was the winter I learned to love the midge, because it was the winter I fished it most. It was the winter Bud first shared his knowledge, his techniques, and his fly patterns with me—patterns he devised, patterns I now see repeated in fly bins everywhere.

Those gray mornings were almost always filled with hatching midges and rising trout. We began the winter stalking gulpers—fish that held along eddy lines waiting for the mats of insects that had collected there to drift slowly toward them. It was an easy thing to cast a clump imitation—a Griffith's Gnat of large proportions, a #12 or #14—into a pile of naturals that was caught in the eddy, to wait for it to drift with the spiraling current toward a feeding trout, to watch the trout's mouth open to take in the bugs, to lift the rod and feel the weight of a good fish.

The quantity of food available to trout during such a hatch is incredible—each gulp contains dozens of insects. Trout feeding this way will often munch on the floating raft of insects, taking mouthful after mouthful. It looks and sounds as if the fish are taking bites out of an apple.

It was a time I will not soon forget, laden with vivid memories. Until you have seen and heard trout feeding that way it is hard to imagine, and the presence of falling snow makes it even better. Something about snow falling on the water causes trout to feed with confidence. It is the same confidence that trout exhibit when the wind is blowing and the surface of the water is broken, hiding them from view. However, our view of the fish is not obscured by snow; feeding trout can be seen easily.

We spent many mornings on those snowy days fishing for such trout beneath the sandstone bluffs of the upper river, along the edges, in the swirling eddies behind the big boulders along the riverbank.

We fished for trout that sipped individual midges as well, picky trout that ate tiny insects and winged adult-midge imitations tied on size #26 and #28 hooks.

I assume it is not an isolated phenomenon. I have not experienced it elsewhere, but I have seen it so consistently on the San Juan that I assume it to be widespread. I am speaking of the way trout rise to midges in the presence of falling snow. On those days when the wind is calm and large snowflakes settle slowly onto the river, on days when midges are thick between flakes that turn to slush on the surface as big fish feed, the trout don't rise with their normal, gentle lift of the head—tipping slightly upward to sip and then downward to drift beneath the surface. You don't see dorsal fins or the tips of tails breaking the surface of the water as they rise. You don't watch as fins disappear after a fly has been taken. You can't see fins or tails at all; instead, you see only snouts, mouths, and eyes. The trout rise vertically, their faces puncturing the surface, pointing straight up into the sky, as they grab flies. They bob like buoys in a stormy sea.

In the gray water, gray fishheads bob up and down grabbing gray flies beneath a moody gray sky. There is no color, little sound, and if you fish for a time without grabbing a trout with your tiny hook, the combination of falling snow, flowing water, intense concentration, and gray-sameness combine to create a feeling of vertigo, falling, disorientation. All of these feelings are shattered instantly in the suddenness of a hooked fish—an explosion of water, a bent rod, and a gyrating reel.

The feeling can be shattered more quietly by the discovery, through the gray, that you are not alone, that another angler has come to share the river.

More often than not during that season of gray, snowy days spent fuss-ing over midging trout, that other angler was Neill, and as often as not his appearance would be announced by the sound of a reel that twirled madly, giving up line to a large trout. His presence would be confirmed in the vision of a bundled-up fisherman whose head was hidden beneath the hood of a heavy parka, an obviously skilled angler whose arms were raised, hanging onto a rod that was deeply bowed. You didn't have to see the face to know it was Neill. His style was his alone.

There were many days during that winter when I was able to feel that the San Juan River had become a private club with only three members: Bud, Neill, and myself.

When *Trout* magazine did its issue on the best trout streams in America several years back, Ed Engle, who was then living in southwestern Colorado, wrote about the Dolores River and the San Juan. Neill was the guy he chose to mention in his writing about those rivers—Neill, who had named many of the pools on the Dolores, and who seemed to know each of its big cut-throat by name. Neill was an angler's angler, a meticulous technician, and a man of obsessive passions.

Bud and Neill had been friends. They shared a house at one time. Each had been, in turn, the president of the local Trout Unlimited chapter. They fished together. They spent many an evening together throwing down a few beers and tossing out tall tales. But they had a falling out over a matter of principle. The details of their dispute have become somewhat hazy with the passage of time, but the situation that existed on the river that winter is as clear to me today as it was then: these two fine fishermen who had so much in common and who had shared so many days together on the stream had not spoken for years.

Day after day, Bud and I fished the river. Day after day, Neill fished, too.

The snow kept falling and the midges kept hatching. With Bud's help, I learned to wait until a trout closed its mouth and began to sub-merge before striking—because those tiny hooks pulled free of open mouths. I learned to strike deliberately, but with a short stroke, in order to keep from straightening the fine wire. I learned to keep my line under control, to take up every last bit of unnecessary slack so that such a strike would be possible. I also discovered the wisdom of a statement Tom Montgomery had made to me in Montana: "When you are casting well, your fly seems to materialize on the water where you are looking; you don't have to search for it." If you cannot do that with midges on a gray day, you never find the fly. I discovered the reason why the British continue to make carefully machined, click-drag fly reels: because they work. I found that nothing protects a fine tippet and a small hook as well as such a reel mated to a rod with a supple tip. I discovered that nothing is more welcome on a gray day than the refined sound of such a reel being unwound by a strong fish. I learned the truth of something Datus Proper had written: once you learn to tie a good knot, you realize that the weak link in a midge rig is not the 7X or 8X tippet—it's the hook.

For that entire winter, Bud and I fished in the snow. We fished midges in the upper water even though there were days when we were certain that trout would be rising to mayflies a few miles downstream. If we walked past Neill's parked car when we arrived, we did so without saying a word. Often we would see his unmistakable form across the river, hanging on to a runaway trout.

~

The most crowded part of the San Juan River, as anyone who has fished it knows, is an area called the Kittie Pool. It is a place where people who don't know the river go to fish because it is impossible to get lost there. It is the water you walk into if you follow the trail that goes directly to the river from the main parking lot.

People fish the Kittie Pool because it is close to the parking lot, people fish it because it is easy to wade, and people fish it because it is full of trout. The area contains some excellent water in addition to the run that is the Kittie Pool proper. Islands of willow separate the river into braids. Small runs alternate with broad, shallow flats. Between the Kittie Pool and the main branch of the river—a deep roaring run beneath a sandstone bluff, a run that some call The Back Bowls—there is a beaver pond surrounded by tall willows.

Serious fishermen pooh-pooh this water, and some macho types ridicule anyone who would fish it, but I'll let you in on a little secret: in the winter, when it snows and no one else is on the water, there is nowhere on earth better for fishing dry flies to midging trout. I have spent hours throwing #28 Griffith's Gnats and midge emergers to lunkers that held against the bank, across difficult currents in the beaver pond. I have thrown these same artificials into the chop of the run between the pond and the Kittie Pool, searching the broken water for barely detectable rises to impossibly tiny flies—and I have enjoyed it immensely.

If the truth is told, it is water that Neill loved, too. Neill had the skill and knowledge to take fish anywhere on the river, but in the winter he fished there. It was often the case during that winter of obsession that Bud and I would find ourselves fishing the Beaver Pond, lost in concentration, and we would be drawn out of the vertigo of gray water and falling snow, of bobbing trout and drifting specks we knew to be flies, by the sound of Neill's reel, by the sight of his hunched gray figure casting, hooking, and landing trout.

One March day, for no apparent reason after a winter of complete silence, Bud shouted across the water to Neill, "Hey, Neill, are you fishing dries?"

And Neill answered, "Always."

It was as if two mutes had spoken. I don't know what prompted Bud to question Neill, although I suspect that his generosity of spirit finally overcame his anger at whatever had happened. I don't know why Neill answered; perhaps his stubborn adherence to principle had finally been replaced by warm memories of friendship. Had they spent the winter dancing around each other like a couple of mating prairie chickens, hoping this would finally happen? Had they realized all winter that the silence had lasted far too long? Had the shared bond of the river, the sport, and the years of companionship finally conspired to end their silence? I don't really know. I only know that

Bud called to Neill as if it were the most natural thing in the world, and Neill answered.

We stopped fishing and walked over as Neill was releasing a fine rainbow. He showed us a gorgeous little four-weight that he had just wrapped. We each took a turn throwing it. We admired its delicacy and the beauty of its construction. Not a word was spoken about the past. It was as if the anger of their falling out had melted with the snow in the trout-filled water of the river.

We said good-bye. Bud and I walked back to the car. I don't know that I've ever seen him so content. He said it was the fishing.

Although I still enjoy the river in winter, it has never again been the obsession it once was. And no season since has ever seemed quite so gray.

POACHERS

SOMETIMES IT SEEMS as if Bud's mission in life is to get me killed. This is a bit self-centered, I know. From Bud's perspective the times when he's put my life in jeopardy must seem few indeed. Few, perhaps, but they loom large from where I sit. For a while, before we both went to work as ski instructors at Purgatory—the big ski resort in our neck of the woods—I worked for Bud, who was the ski school director at a smaller ski area just west of Durango. I had never skied at Hesperus before I went to work there, and Bud decided to take me on a tour my first morning on the hill. It had been a year of little snow and I wondered how good the skiing was going to be at a ski area on a mesa that rose barely a thousand feet above the surrounding ranches along Lightner Creek. We rode the chairlift together to the top, and Bud spoke excitedly about the wonders of this grossly underrated place. "There are chutes here that will pucker your asshole, Steve."

He was right. I stayed puckered all morning. My good friend Hollis, whose boy Jake skis a lot like my son, Daniel, once told me that the three most dangerous words on the mountain are "Follow me, Daddy!" I have learned that those words could be changed a little and still be dangerous— as in "Follow me, Steve," when uttered by Bud.

Our first run was down a wide boulevard called Lone Pine that would have been a lovely dance down an open thirty-degree slope if not for the fact that the twenty-inch snowpack failed to cover the twenty-one-inch stubble of chain saw–cut scrub oak. Every turn found the tails of our skies snagged in brush, and the only way to survive was to cut extremely shallow arcs that did little to control our speed on the steep slope. When we arrived at the bottom, Bud was beaming with excitement. I was faint with the adrenaline rush of near-death. It went ever more steeply downhill from there.

We skied narrow gullies less than a turn wide. We skied sandstone outcroppings with forced carries onto more scrub-oak stubble. Bud flew and I struggled to keep up. And always he beamed. I shouldn't have been surprised; it's been like this with Bud from the first time we did anything together.

We spent our first fishing trip together crawling around on our hands and knees, poaching on a little creek that flowed through a cattle ranch near Dallas Divide. I certainly don't want to condone poaching or trespassing on private property. Lord knows, there are enough bumper stickers displayed to remind us to "Ask first to hunt or fish on private land!" But I don't know a serious fisherman who hasn't crossed a fence sometime in his life.

There were plenty of ways to rationalize our behavior that day: there weren't any cattle present, and the rancher wouldn't have to worry about us running any weight off his stock or turning them loose by leaving gates open—we don't leave gates open; we weren't going to kill any trout, just exercise a few, then put them back; we hadn't actually walked through any no trespassing signs or notices that the land was posted. But there was no way around it: if you walk through a gate or climb over a fence, you should get permission first.

We were on our way back from a particularly depressing Wildlife Commissioners meeting in Grand Junction, a carefully orchestrated meeting where a couple of well-rehearsed, teary-eyed actors had spoken with weak, quavering voices about the terrible sadness of not seeing any minorities, any little kids or families, on the elitist fly-and-lure-only water that has become the home of yuppies and wealthy urbanites who wear British woolens and fish with rods that cost a whole hell of a lot more than the $19.95 wondersticks they have to use. They cried about the fact that the water they were forced to fish (probably a thousand times as much water as the protected water they coveted) didn't have any big fish. They said it was racist and discriminatory to give all those big fish to the rich fly fishermen. Bud and I just sat there and shook our heads. We weren't feeling particularly wealthy at the time. We had driven to the meeting in Bud's car—a twenty-year-old Mercury Capri he had bought from a friend for a few bucks. It ran pretty good but had no dashboard or exterior paint (the Western sun had long since turned them to powder)—and we'd brought along a few peanut butter sandwiches because we couldn't afford to eat in a restaurant. We were damned mad about the fact that there had once been a hell of a lot of good water in this state before half of it was buried beneath reservoirs, and the rest either fished out or ruined by industrial, agricultural, and urban poison.

There are still a few good fish left, and this meeting conjured up images of this noble remnant lying ingloriously in state collecting freezer burn, or being thrown unceremoniously into the trash after being shown to a few buddies down at work. Where did these whiners think all the big fish had gone? Many of them had gone into the very freezers and garbage cans of those same poor, sad fishermen who were crying to get the regs lifted so they could ruin the rest of the water in the state. And it looked, for a while, as if they might pull it off. It is hard to resist an appeal on the grounds of elitism and racism, no matter how falsely conceived or cynically calculated.

It turned out that this whole charade had been arranged by a wealthy "sportsman" from the Front Range who just happened to like killing big fish. Fortunately, it didn't work.

On the drive back, we passed Dallas Creek. With a twinkle in his eye, Bud said, "I've heard there are some pretty good fish in there."

We spent what little light was left crawling around on our hands and knees, partly to keep from startling the trout, and partly to keep from getting an unwanted load of rock salt shotgunned up our butts by an irate rancher.

We raised a few good browns that refused our bushy dry flies, and we managed to land a couple of smaller fish that we released back into the creek. We were poaching.

But there's poaching and there's poaching, and the time I most nearly met death with Bud, it was not because we were trespassing on private water, it was because someone else was poaching on water that we felt pretty strongly about, and because something snapped inside when Bud saw serious poachers—real poachers—throwing three- to five-pound rainbows from the San Juan into the willows to be loaded into coolers and taken home.

~

It was winter, and we had grown used to having the river to ourselves. It was the season when I came as close as any in my life to being a true trout bum. I'd had a few winters when I was younger when I'd skied enough (and ignored everything else) to think of myself as a ski bum. I'd spent months fishing every day, still managing to hold down a full-time job. But this winter was different. I'd lost my wife to leukemia the previous fall, and nothing much mattered. I threw myself into the river to drown my grief, and in the process discovered a pretty fair route to healing. But I didn't know that at the time. All I knew was that, for some reason, I needed to be fishing all the time, and work seemed quite unimportant to me.

Bud was healing his own wounds. He had suffered his own losses—a divorce, financial difficulty—and he, too, had turned to rivers to find his rhythm again.

Although we usually fished by ourselves, that blustery day we went down to the San Juan with a good friend, Dave Culver. Dave was in no way a trout bum, although I suspect it is an option he eyes with some seriousness every now and then. He's a psychologist with a good practice. He is also a man with a lot of good friends. I know few comments about a person that mean as much.

It was a rare day on the river for Dave, and we were happy to have him with us.

We entered the water below the stilling basin, a few hundred yards downstream from the dam. There was a trout holding in the clear water about fifteen feet beyond the place where the trail meets the river. The spot is marked by a tripod of pipe. The rising trout was an old friend. All winter we had seen him there, holding against the bottom or rising to midges. He greeted us as warmly as the sun coming over the bluffs, as reliably as the river itself that became visible when we emerged from the trail and the willows to meet the open water.

Unspoken rituals and courtesies grow around friends who fish often together. I would not fish parts of the Florida River without Bud. It is his home water, and I feel that I am a guest there. Although we have never spoken about it, I know that there is water on Lime Creek that Bud would never fish without me. I tie classic wet flies for Bud when we fish the creeks because I love to tie them, and I know that he loves to fish them. Bud ties Hare's Ears for me because he knows that I would rather fish one of his Hare's Ears than anyone else's—or even my own. It's not as if I couldn't fish the Florida without him, or that he couldn't do well on my home water without me. It isn't that either one of us needs the other to tie flies. These are courtesies, not necessities—small gestures that indicate a much larger reservoir of respect and friendship.

That fish—the one that always rose just beyond the tripod—was Bud's. I would no more have thought of throwing a fly at it than I would of moving into his house without his permission. He had been watching that fish every day he fished the upper river since first spotting it, and it was our custom for Bud either to try for that fish or tip his hat and move on.

That day we paused for a moment on our way across the river, before searching the runs beneath the bluffs, so Bud could cast to that trout.

The run below the stilling basin is a broad glide, perhaps two hundred feet across. The bottom appears almost perfectly uniform, covered with fist-sized river rock and smaller gravel. The water is a nearly constant, mid-thigh depth, but if you look closely, you will discover an occasional bucket, a deeper place where a trout will sometimes hold out of the current, snatching underwater food. Sometimes they rise from the buckets to feed on the surface, and that is exactly what Bud's trout was doing. It held inches beneath the surface, tipping its nose upward occasionally to take a clump of midges.

Bud sat at river's edge and tied a length of 7X tippet to his leader. To the tippet he tied a #26 midge-clump. Then he rose to cast—gentle, slow rolling loops—out toward the feeding trout, his old friend. Although the fish was rising fairly regularly, a few minutes of casting the clump over its nose brought no strike and we decided to move on.

The three of us worked our way across the river, and took positions beneath the bluff where we positioned ourselves at hundred-yard intervals, casting midge pupae into a run that was full of nymphing trout.

The day was cold and wet. A bitter wind blew from the southwest carrying the moisture of a Pacific storm. Snow squalls came and went. The water changed with each squall from table-flat and glass-clear to whitecap-rough and obscure. We fished through squall and calm, in sight of each other.

The morning passed with a good number of trout raised and hooked. The fishing kept us warm, to a point, but around noon, we were chilled and ready for lunch. We left the run we were fishing to walk back across the river to the car and, as we were walking, Bud noticed a couple of guys who were fishing with spinning rods up by the dam.

"I don't like the looks of that," he said.

As we got closer we could see that they were throwing the fish they caught behind them into the willows. Bud became livid.

I continued walking. Bud began stomping. We arrived at the tripod, but there was no trout rising in the river; instead, we found the fish gasping for oxygen in a muddy puddle above the bank where the poachers had dropped it, hoping to keep it fresh until they could come back and claim their booty. Bud saw this old friend and adversary struggling for breath in the stagnant water, rolling on its side, unable to maintain equilibrium. Very slowly, very gently, he lifted the fish and carried it to the river, where he began to revive it. I could see his anger building toward explosion.

Just before Bud released the trout, he screamed upriver to the bastards who were murdering fish, "Hey you sonsabitches, you killing fish?!"

One of them shouted back, "No!"

Bud lifted the trout he had been reviving, and yelled, full of rage, "Then what the hell is this?!"

It is a short ride from grief to anger; it is a small step from introspection to violence—especially when sanctuary has been invaded by vandals. It was as if a monastic retreat had been violated. Not only had a place of healing been defiled, but friends were being murdered. I can find no other explanation for the rage I saw in Bud's eyes. I felt that rage as well, but I doubt I would have attacked if I had been there by myself. There's no doubt in my mind what Bud would have done, alone or with twenty companions.

Bud moved off at a trot toward the poachers, and I struggled to keep up. I couldn't let him arrive in front of the poachers alone—there were two of them, and poachers can be nasty.

When we got there, Bud began screaming obscenities at a thick-necked guy who was built like a linebacker, and as he screamed, with me standing behind him for moral support—lending him all the authority of a thin frame that no amount of winter clothing could disguise—the poacher's buddy came up, then three more appeared from the willows. There were five of them. They were all big, they were all seething, and each had a sheath knife on his belt the size of a machete.

Well, this is it, I thought, *Hoka hey, it's a good day to die.* Maybe we would go down, but we would sure take a couple of them with us, and it would be worth it.

Bud and the tough guy with the big neck stuck their red faces together, and with veins popping kept screaming at each other, yelling words I choose not to record. I kept a mean eye on the others and they did the same to me.

But no blow was ever struck.

In the madness of the moment, I had forgotten completely about Dave—so intense was the anger, so immediate the vein-popping, face-against-face, screaming argument. But Dave had not forgotten us, and he continued to walk across the river and amble over to see if he might lend a hand.

Dave is what you might call large. I'd guess six eight. And he's not skinny, he's kind of solid. He carries the kind of quiet authority that says, "The reason I'm not losing my cool is because I'm pretty sure of myself, and I think you'd be making a big mistake to screw with me." He never said a word; he just kept walking toward the verbal melee. I watched as the loudmouthed poacher took his hand off the handle of his knife, took his face out of Bud's, lowered his volume about a hundred decibels, and mumbled something like: "Well we didn't know you couldn't keep fish here."

The others backed away a little and looked at the ground, shuffling their feet.

That was bull, and we all knew it—signs listing the special regulations are posted all along the river—but in matters of brinkmanship and what had now become the negotiation of disengagement, it passed for truth. No more fish were slaughtered that day, and no humans joined them.

~

The following spring, I was guiding a party of two—an elderly couple from the Deep South—on a beautiful, balmy afternoon. The warm breeze was soft, and there was a scent of sage in the air. Rainbows were rising to Baetis. Our conversation was gentle.

Our reverie was shattered by the sound of a guide, downriver, who was shouting at a couple of ill-mannered brutes who had dead fish hanging from their belts—dead fish paraded about on a stretch of no-kill water!

"Oh my," the sweet lady asked, "what's that?"

"Poachers," I replied. "Poachers having a discussion with a good friend of mine. Maybe I'll introduce you to him. Later."

THE WATER WITCH

HIGH WATER, on most freestone rivers and on many tailwaters, is a time to fish somewhere else. Rivers that seem almost creek-like in summer become big, ugly flows. The water turns opaque and the trout hug the bottom. Big, heavily weighted nymphs, crystal-flash scuds, rabbit leeches, and worms with fluorescent bands are used to pound fish up from the bottom. It is a kind of fishing I can tolerate for a few days, if necessary, but a steady diet of such monotony soon kills my desire to go fishing.

In recent years the periods of high water on the San Juan have been difficult times to fish, and the length of time that the river remains murky seems much longer than it used to. Such annual rhythms are difficult to decipher and hard to predict, but few would argue with the notion that, lately, high water on the San Juan is not as pleasant as it was a few years ago.

In the past, high water brought drifting vegetation and murkiness for a few days or weeks but the debris in the water soon settled out, and the river cleared. Channels through the willows that had been dirt-covered paths at low water became clear, shallow streams. The fish migrated into these many miles of newly formed channels in order to escape the powerful currents of the main river.

We used to look forward to high water because it scared away a great many timid waders, created miles of unmolested water, and because it made for some of the best fishing of the year. But recent high flows have brought with them dirty water that lasts for month after distressing month.

~

Last year, after many weeks of elevated flows, after months of patient searching for trout with weighted leaders in dismal water, fishing with nymphs that sometimes imitated food but more often imitated nothing so much as a bright object that might draw attention from an invisible trout, I crossed the heavy current of the main channel at the head of the Texas Hole with Mike Crowley. Mike and I had a suspicion that the channels near the upper islands might hold some good-sized fish.

There was no way to get a boat to them. The boat ramps were all down-stream and there was no way to launch one above the islands. Rowing up the channel was out of the question. We hadn't been able to wade into the area from the south side—the road side—of the river. We hoped the water around the islands might be accessible from the bluffs along the north side, but we needed to cross the dangerous water of the main channel. We decided to use Mike's drift boat to cross at the Texas Hole, then hike upriver along the bluffs.

Mike is a big man, and a powerful wader. A few weeks earlier I had spent a few days hiking and fishing in the Black Canyon with him. We had taken a boat that day, too—not Mike's big drift boat, but one of my small, light canoes. The trail we used to get to the river allowed access to very little water. A few hundred yards either side of the trail, the canyon walls grew vertical, and there was no way to move upstream or down. The water of the Gunnison River flows through the canyon, pinched by the narrow walls of a 2,500-foot-deep Precambrian gorge. Huge boulders fill the riverbed. Broad, deep pools alternate with powerful rapids. Much of the stretch we fished is unnavigable to even the most skilled kayakers, and swimming it would mean certain drowning. The attraction of the gorge for fishermen is the fact that the fish there have seen precious few flies or lures.

The water is full of browns and rainbows that have grown to good size. The canoe allowed us to cross the river by ferrying one of the calm pools, and from the other side we were able to hike and fish over a mile of river without company, except for ravens, peregrines, and ringtails.

For the most part, I fished within a few feet of shore. But Mike, at six-foot five and well over two hundred pounds, with the grace of a superb athlete, easily waded runs that would have dragged me under and killed me for sure. We had an extraordinary trip, taking some beautiful trout from the powerful water; but the best part of the trip for me, apart from the incredible beauty of the canyon itself, was the pleasure of watching Mike wade and fish that awesome river.

So I expected much the same when we got to the islands of the San Juan that spring day of heavy murky water. Mike was going to cross a channel that I knew I would never manage. I would fish from the bluff side. We hoped we would find good trout.

Mike worked his way out into the river, and even though he was crossing a channel that he had waded a thousand times at low water, he moved with great caution in the now-heavy current. The water climbed up his waders, first to his knees, then his thighs, and finally to his hips. He said nothing, but kept working toward the islands. When the water reached his chest, his feet went out from under him, and he went in. Swimming strongly, whooping loudly in the icy water—aided a bit, perhaps, by the fact that he was wearing buoyant neoprene waders—he was able to reach the island, soaked and cold, but in a position to fish.

He pulled off his clothes and hung them on willows to dry. Standing before me across the hundred-foot channel wearing nothing but underpants, boots, and a vest, he began to nymph the water patiently.

~

I have heard it said that there are two kinds of fishermen. I believe that there is some of each of them in all of us, but we definitely tend toward one kind or the other: there are people who fish the water and people who fish to fish.

It has become significantly more popular to fish to fish on rivers where they can be seen. The efficiency of this kind of angling cannot be doubted. Neither can the pleasures. But I sometimes wonder if there is something bigger going on here than preference.

At one time, most of us fished for trout on streams where they often did not show themselves. Some of the best books on fishing were written by experts at fishing the water. Ray Bergman's legendary *Trout* is just such a book, and I spent many years patiently putting my fly through the water that Ray had told me to fish. I cast in order: first short, then longer, careful not to disturb any of the places where a trout was likely to be (even though I had not seen one) with a wayward shadow, clumsy step, or poorly placed fly line. I cast beneath undercut banks and overhanging willows, around large boulders. I hooked fish in places where they were supposed to be, and sometimes in places where they were not supposed to be, and if I fished a stream often enough I came to feel the places where they might be hiding, the places where a fly would have a good chance of connecting with an unseen trout.

I developed fish sense, and I acquired what little of it I have the hard way: through trial and error.

But I believe there are some who are born with it, some who walk into the water knowing where the fish are. In the same way that many anglers feel the presence of fish in water that they know, or water that is similar to a place they know, some people arrive at a piece of water the likes of which they have never seen and immediately locate trout. It appears that they are fishing the water, but my guess is that they are often fishing to fish.

There are people who will tell you that fishing is a simple matter of science, not magic; biology, not intuition. It would go against everything written in the how-to press to argue otherwise, and I would never attempt to do so. There is no question that the science of fly fishing has grown tremendously. As we have learned their habits we have steadily taken more trout, and more difficult trout. In fishing, as in questions of faith and philosophy, however, when skill and knowledge are a given and the limits are pushed, when excellence is assumed and transcendent greatness becomes the issue, long after the ninety-ninth percentile has been reached and we find ourselves in the company of extraordinary people or extraordinary anglers, science dissolves and miracles occur.

~

A few winters ago, so late at night it was hard to decide whether it was yesterday or tomorrow, whether I was dreaming or awake, I was pulled from a deep sleep by the sound of water running in my basement. Fearful that a frozen pipe had burst, I jumped out of bed and bounced down the steep stairs with a flashlight. The sound grew louder with every step, but there was no water. I pointed the flashlight into corners, swept the floor with the yellow beam, and saw only the dusty cement pad of a small cellar, the dry brown dirt of the crawl space beyond. But the sound was unmistakable. Running water. I put my ear against the water main, and the sound became deafening.

I grabbed a coat, pulled on some boots, and walked out into the yard, this time sweeping the frozen ground with the light, looking for water that might be percolating up from a broken feedline. Nothing.

When I got to the street I found what I was looking for. The crack between the concrete curb and the asphalt pavement had been obliterated. In its place rose a high-pressure wall of water, falling away inches from where the crack should have been to run southward, downhill, much like the upwelling source, the dome of water where a large underground spring feeds a spring creek. Below the gush, the street had become a river.

I ran inside, called the water department, and within minutes a small white pickup arrived in front of my house. There was only one man in the truck. Our street has no streetlights, and the lights of the truck had been turned off, but a bright winter moon illuminated the inside of the cab and I could see that the person who had come was an elderly Hispanic man with white hair and mustache. His shiny dark skin glowed in the moonlight. He stepped from the truck holding a piece of wire coat hanger bent into the shape of a Y. He held it in his hands like a turkey wishbone—one hand on each leg, the single stem pointing forward—and proceeded to walk the length of the street above the place where water was pouring from the pavement. As he did, his coat hanger jerked down. He spray-painted a white line on the pavement. Then he walked across the street and back toward his mark, and as he neared the line he had just painted, his coat hanger jerked down again. He crossed the first line with another stripe of paint, making an X. It took mere seconds. He smiled at me, said good morning, and drove off.

Hours later, a large crew arrived to assess the rupture, which by now had turned several people's yards into marshland and the intersection downhill from it into a lake. Three big trucks full of young engineers wearing hard hats rumbled to a halt. They emerged carrying books and maps. One of the trucks was a huge van that bristled with antennae. When the side door was opened, I looked inside. The van was full of electronic equipment. Cathode-ray screens glowed with an eerie green light. Computers clicked and whirred. The equipment and the personnel seemed more appropriate for suspected terrorist sabotage, or Martian invasion, than a simple pipe break.

One of the hard hats began dropping transponders on the street—in neighbors' yards, in my own yard—following a chart that he held in his hand. When I looked again at the glowing screen, I realized that it was an electronic map of the neighborhood with the routes of the pipes that lay underground plotted carefully. Superimposed upon this map, now that the transponders had been put in place, was a wavy line that showed the point of maximum noise. Another of the hard hats left the van with a can of blue spray paint, and proceeded to mark the pavement twenty feet away from the spot that had been painted earlier by the elderly gentleman who had walked the street with a bent coat hanger.

A backhoe was called up and began to dig where the blue X had been painted. Slowly the machine worked its way down through the pavement, the gravel, the rich, brown dirt and boulders of the roadbed, until it came to the main water pipe.

No leak.

Slowly the backhoe tore up more street. Slowly it dug through the layers. Slowly it worked its way down toward the white X that had been ignored by the hard hats and the engineers, the guys in the van who had the glowing screen that showed the noise as a wavy line on a perfect map. When they got to the white X they dug, once again, through the pavement, through the gravel, through the rich brown dirt and the boulders, when suddenly the ground exploded with mud and water. They had found the leak.

The engineers drove away, and a crew of road workers appeared to deal with the mess. I told one of them what had happened—about the old man with the white hair and the coat hanger, about the monster van and the electronic gizmos, about the two Xs, and where the leak had been found. He just smiled at me and laughed.

"Those young kids—the ones with the engineering degrees—they never listen to the old guy. He knows everything. He knows where the pipes are. He knows when the maps are wrong. He knows where the leaks are. He can smell 'em. I don't know what we're going to do when he retires."

I have no doubt they'll still be able to find the leaks. They'll still have the big van with the antennae. They'll still have their hard hats and their engineering degrees and, like many purely scientific fishermen with profound knowledge and a lot of good tackle, sooner or later they'll hook into the big one. Some guys just need a coat hanger—or an old fly rod—and instinct.

For most of us the odds improve with knowledge and better tackle, but I've been in the company of water witches and I know that no amount of study or gear will ever be able to compete with a gift; and if I had the choice, which unfortunately I don't, I'd rather be a witch than an expert.

~

A few seasons ago, I took a friend fishing. Linda was relatively new to fly fishing, but there was no question that she had the passion. She loved to fish and wanted to learn more. I met her seven years ago, when my second wife

was very sick, and we have been friends ever since. Linda was one of the
nurses who cared for my wife before her death, and I came to realize during
the long, sad course of the disease that, when serious illness strikes, medical
care is delivered by nurses. Doctors hurried in and out of our lives at that
time, and my memory of most of them has become a blur. With few exceptions, however, I remember the nurses as if it were yesterday.

Linda is a gifted nurse. Her knowledge is voluminous and her clinical
skills are extraordinary, but her real talent is her instinct. She seems to know
what you are feeling before you tell her. She can fill in the blanks between
what you know enough to ask, the fears you cannot quite articulate. Every
time she walked into the room during those terrible days, she brought genuine concern, the resources to help, and a comforting assurance and calm
that eased pain better than any medication.

I knew a few other things about Linda before we went fishing that day,
and they added to my belief that she was likely to do anything she attempted
with more skill and grace than others. She had an ease and naturalness about
her that made difficult things appear easy. For example, I have watched her
ski horrid, choppy moguls on steep runs with flimsy telemark skis and soft
leather boots, her long blond ponytail bouncing behind her, a huge grin on
her face, as others struggled desperately to keep up. My wife, Debbie, has
ridden horseback with her through dense woods and mountain meadows.
She tells me that Linda rides like the wind, in perfect balance, fearless, gal-
loping her ecstatic horse through terrain that would terrify ordinary riders.
There is no vanity in her, no sense of competition. She genuinely enjoys such
things, and it seems as if she has no idea how remarkable she is.

But her fishing technique was a little rough the day we first went down
to the San Juan. She had not yet spent much time casting on big water (most
of her fishing had been on small creeks). She had never seen a mend, or been
told about the need for nymphs to drift naturally with the current. She had
never fished extremely small flies or fine tippets. All of these skills would
need honing before she would take fish consistently on the San Juan. Or so
I thought.

We ran into another good friend in the parking lot and decided to fish together. George, who joined us, was an accomplished fisherman—no question about it. He was well read, well practiced, and he had good tackle. He'd fished a lot of tough water, and he spent a fair amount of time on the stream. He was active in trout conservation and well known in local angling circles. He was good, but he was no witch.

We worked our way out into a shallow flat with a moderately fast current tongue at its head. We rigged with midge pupae and began casting. I showed Linda how to mend, and within a cast or two she was fast to a screaming trout. That one broke her after a powerful run, but she quickly landed a few others, and seemed—always—to be into fish. George and I were thrilled at her success and passed loud congratulations as she continued to fish.

Standing next to Linda, not casting, I fed her information about her drifts, about the likely places to find trout. I should have saved my breath; she didn't need the help. She cast where she wanted, and she cast where she thought there ought to be a fish. Remember: she had never taken a fish on the river before.

But she took them that day. She took them from the current seam where I told her to cast. She took them in the middle of the heavy water where I had never seen them before. She took them with a regularity that was astonishing. And it wasn't long before the few others within sight of us left. George fell silent. Suddenly it struck me that no one else had as much as hooked a fish since our arrival, and I later heard that no one was catching any before we got there. There was no hatch on, and I hadn't put her in that water so much to take fish as to get her warmed up for the time when the fish would begin to feed. Apparently she didn't know it was a poor time to catch fish.

George grew more intense. He cast with greater concentration, and with the most deliberate technique I have ever seen. Cast after cast went into good water. Cast after cast he mended perfectly. Cast after unmolested cast he struck at the end of the drift—hoping to feel the weight of a fish even though there had been no indication that he had any reason to hope for one—before picking up his line to try again. Meanwhile, not fifty feet away from his deliberate and most excellent angling, Linda was giggling with glee as she merrily played trout after trout.

The supreme insult occurred late in the day. Still fishless, George continued to dredge the water. Linda had stopped fishing to get something from her vest. She stuck her rod between her knees and fumbled with her pockets. Her line dangled, out of control, beneath her. Suddenly she began to shriek.

"Steeeeve! Oh, Jeez! Oh, my God! Hey look at this! Steve, I caught one with the rod between my knees!"

It was too much for George. He stomped from the water, threw his rod into the willows, and stormed off. I don't blame him. It would have been pretty hard to take, and I imagine I might have done the same thing if I hadn't been laughing so hard. Deep down, though, I knew that it wasn't funny. It was humbling. It always is when you're in the presence of that kind of natural ability.

Linda has the gift.

~

Writers like Ray Bergman wrote from that gift. Sometimes, in cynical moments, I wonder if much of what passes for expertise in this sport isn't really compensation for the lack of that gift. If you fish long enough, you figure out whether you've got it or not. I don't. But sometimes I fall into it for a moment or two. On water I have fished a thousand times, I am given a glimpse of what it must be like. Sometimes it comes to me on new water and I fish in a temporary state of grace.

That day of heavy water, with Mike, was such a day. Even through the murk I could sense them. Even beneath the raging current I could feel their presence. Drift after deep drift was intercepted, as I knew it would be, by a huge rainbow. None was smaller than three pounds. Many were considerably larger.

The brilliant orange light of late afternoon bathed the cliffs behind me. It was a holy scene, an Ottoman panel dazzling with gold leaf, a precious moment in the life history of one of the long-suffering but ever-faithful saints. Seraphim danced in the willows. Mike had been transformed into some kind of grotesque cherub in underpants by the awesome power of the river.

Mike—who always outfishes me with the most gentle graciousness—could only stand in mute adoration on a distant shore as the cataclysmic apocalypse unfolded and the meek inherited the earth.

SOME DAYS ARE ELECTRIC

THE BUGS OF WINTER have little variety. In midwinter there are midges: small midges and smaller midges. Black midges, gray midges, and olive-green midges. The pupae are mostly black and olive. The larvae are usually white, yellow, or dark green. There are leeches and worms. (We call the worms annelids now to distinguish ourselves from bait fishermen.) Various macro-invertebrates bide their time among the silts, gravels, and boulders—occasionally finding themselves caught in the current and thus becoming trout food. But winter, by and large, is a time of midges.

In late winter the first mayflies begin to appear. They are the har-bingers of spring, and their appearance means that there will be more dry-fly fishing in the months ahead. These early mayflies are the blue-winged olives. They come in various shades of gray and olive and range from a size #18 down to #24. Although the insects in this group come from two distinct genuses (*Baetis* and *Pseudocloeon*), several species of both are commonly referred to by anglers as *Baetis*. A third group of Baetidae—the Callibaetis, or speckle-winged dun—also provides good dry-fly fishing, but its appearance is not as reliable as that of the other Baetidae.

The best hatches of *Baetis* will not come again until fall, but after weeks of cold winter weather and constant midge fishing, the appearance of even a few mayflies is a welcome sight.

Midges hatch throughout the year, and with the exception of a month or two in winter when the *Baetis* are sparse, the gray or olive duns can be seen nearly as often, drifting on the surface of the water, drying their upright wings before taking flight.

Blue-winged olives can appear just about anywhere in the quality water, but one piece of water is named for them, and rightly so. Baetis Bend marks the midpoint of the regulated water. It consists of two parts. The upper part of the bend lies below a small island that marks the lower end of Lunker Lane. Water comes into the bend as a pair of current tongues divided by the island, but soon it flattens out, becoming broad, calm, shallow, and clear. The gravel bar that marks the lower end of this pool drops abruptly into the deeper water of the lower bend—a wide, curving expanse of river that is lined by high sandstone cliffs. The lower bend is unwadeable. The upper bend is knee to waist deep. It is ideal dry-fly water.

For many years the upper pool of Baetis Bend was my favorite piece of water on the entire river. At one time, *Baetis* hatches were quite predictable. Once they began to appear, daily hatches occurred with precision. In early spring the hatch would come off each day between one and two in the afternoon and end an hour or so later. As the season progressed, the hatch would begin a few minutes earlier and last a few minutes longer each day until midsummer, when the hatch might begin at eleven in the morning and continue until late in the afternoon. Or so I remember it. These spring and summer hatches have become less predictable in recent years, and the trout of Baetis Bend have changed as well. A few years ago, however, it was some of the best dry-fly water I have ever experienced. Some days produced fishing beyond belief. Some days were positively electric.

The rhythm of a Baetis hatch on the San Juan is very much like that of the hatch of this insect on other Western rivers. An hour or so before the appearance of duns, fish begin to show themselves in the places where the adult insects will hatch. Nymphs become active in deep water and work their way gradually to the surface. The fish move with them, starting near the bottom and gradually rising to the top. Chocolate-brown Hare's Ears, various black, olive, and gray nymphs in size #18 or #20, will take fish when drifted without drag and with a little lead on the leader. As the fish move closer to the surface, winged patterns become more effective and can be fished with less lead. Just before the duns appear, trout can be taken in the film with emergers—Harrop Transition Duns, CDC emergers, and floating nymphs all work. Finally, at the peak of the hatch, when the water is covered with dimpling trout and sheets of adult insects, the trout become susceptible to dry flies. Gray and olive Sparkle Duns have become quite popular. Comparaduns are effective. Every now and then a trout will become picky, and fishermen will rummage through various quill-winged no-hackle patterns, parachute duns, or unique, idiosyncratic concoctions to tempt rising fish. I have cast to the dimpling trout of Baetis Bend for many years now, and I have fished all of these flies and more, but my favorite for reasons of obstinacy and tradition remains a muskrat-dubbed, grizzly-and-brown-hackled Thorax Adams. I fish it because I like the way it looks, because it reminds me of Vincent Marinaro, and because it takes fish.

In past years the trout that fed on the olives in Baetis Bend were heavy and relatively untouched. Unlike the trout on some parts of the upper river that fell regularly victim to gaudy worms and large-hooked leaches—trout that often lost mandibles to ham-handed fishermen—the trout of the Bend were usually caught, if they were caught at all, on tiny nymphs and dry flies. Many trout that were held by anglers were completely unmarked. They ran hard when hooked, jumped freely, and often took fishermen into their backing. I remember those days fondly, if a bit sadly now. In recent years the river has been stocked with thousands of small fish, and they have taken up residence in the Bend. I don't know how long they will remain, or if the

fishing will be like it once was when they have grown, or died. I rarely fish
Baetis Bend any more.

Because of this, my memories seem more precious, perhaps even a bit
exaggerated. When I think of hatches there, I remember the days when the
water was covered with insects, the days when the surface of the water was
unruffled by wind, when the water was so clear that you could see the sandy
bottom and against it the dark shapes of large trout. Days in memory are
filled with images of bank-feeding trout and trout in the middle of the pool
that were difficult to tempt, trout that required a good imitation carefully
cast from a long way off. Perhaps the most startling thing about my memories of the hatches in Baetis Bend years ago is the fact that this extraordinary
piece of dry-fly water would often belong just to me and a few good friends.

These memories, of course, have been the beneficiary of time and forgetting. When I try to remember less wonderful things, those images come
as well. There were days, even years ago, when that idyllic scene would be
interrupted by the presence of strangers—strangers who sometimes fished an
orange worm throughout the hatch, strangers who yelled and shouted to
each other from great distances about the "hawg" they had just hooked,
strangers who sometimes lifted heavy trout from the water, carried them to
the bank for photographs, then released these trout in poor condition, some
to die. There were days of wind that blew every dun from the water and kept
the trout from rising. Still, not all of those good memories are dishonest, and
not every perfect day remembered is a delusion. Baetis Bend provided great
fishing and great times with friends, and some days, even when remembered
with perfect clarity and honesty, were exceptional.

About six years ago, I spent an afternoon there with Bud and an
extraordinary angler named Mark Engler. Mark and I scarcely knew each
other then. I saw him often on the river and I had seen few catch as many
fish. I have heard fishermen described as heron-like in their intensity, and
although it has become something of a cliché, this describes Mark perfectly,
both in appearance and behavior. Many times I watched him stand still in the

water, select a target, wait to cast until the right moment, then strike quickly. Nothing else mattered to him in that moment. Not the weather. Not the scenery. Not even the people he was with. There would be plenty of time for that later. In the moment of fishing there was nothing else. I have seen few anglers fish as well.

We were in the Bend, with the pool to ourselves. A hatch of enormous proportions was in progress, and trout broke the surface taking the *Baetis* duns. We stood roughly a hundred feet apart, and none of us needed to move in order to find new targets. Dozens of fish rose within casting range. We fished, casting a few feet above a selected, rising trout, watching as our flies drifted over the fish. Our drifts were short, repetitious, and methodical. There were so many bugs on the water that we had to cover fish repeatedly in order to have any hope of catching them, but we did hook fish regularly, and every trout hooked brought a smile from the others.

Sometimes a fish would be especially heavy—perhaps three or four pounds—and it would run hard. We pushed our 6X tippets to the limit against the light drag of our reels and the added drag of long fly lines trailing behind the fast-running fish. Sometimes a fish would break off, or the fly would come free. Often a trout would come reluctantly into the net and be lifted from the water. It was the kind of fishing we dream about, the kind we remember when we wonder what it is that keeps us fishing after hundreds of days on the stream.

Perhaps that is why we didn't notice the coming storm. Or, if we noticed the building signs, why we chose to pretend that they did not exist. The surface of the water became choppy. The yellow glow that had illuminated the river bottom earlier, that had provided a view of trout suspended in transparent, limpid water, gave way to a steel gray filter that came between us and the fish. Still, we continued to cast and hook trout. Thunder crashed in the distance. Still, we continued to fish.

That world of wind and water, of distant rumbling and flashing, of rising trout that persisted in spite of the chop, of casting and drifting and hooking and playing, was shattered by a blast, by an overwhelming flash of light, by the sound of crackling heard clearly in the explosion, and by the sight of my best friend slumped over in the water, his Powell rod drifting downstream. Bud had been hit by lightning.

I screamed, and now I marvel at the idiocy of my words, "Bud, your rod!" He came out of his stupor, grabbed the rod, and together the three of us staggered from the water. Bud seemed fine, if rattled.

A large bolt of lightning had struck the bluffs high above us, but a side bolt or induced current had rocketed down his graphite rod and into his hand. There was a burn on his thumb where the charge had exited the rod into his body. Miraculously, somehow, he had not been hurt seriously.

Once on shore, we made jokes. We laughed hysterically. We did the things people do to avoid confronting a very real and immediate truth: some-one we cared a great deal about had nearly died. We might all have died. Heron or no, fishing didn't seem terribly important in that moment.

When the storm passed, Mark resumed fishing. I joined him, but my intensity was gone. Bud sat on the bank, dazed.

Since that day, I no longer procrastinate when electrical storms threaten. Now I get out of the water immediately. I find myself wanting to call John Gierach to tell him that there's yet another reason to fish bamboo rods, but I suspect he already knows. I have added a memory of Baetis Bend that is even more remarkable than the others. And I realize, again as I write, that the loss of a friend is a terrible, terrible thing to contemplate.

THE BIG BUG

THE SEASONS ROLL ON. Winter turns into spring and spring into summer, but one constant remains: tiny flies.

I am reminded of a dozen jokes, a dozen stories, that relate the experience of purgatory not to great pain and suffering but to never-ending sameness. G. E. M. Skues's wonderful story, "Mr. Theodore Castwell," captures the horrible feeling perfectly.

Castwell appears before St. Peter after a long, successful sporting life. Quarters are arranged beside a stretch of Test-like spring creek. He is sent to the water in the company of an attending angel. The angel produces a splendid fly rod, reel, line, and leader. Insects are on the water, and fish rise to them. The attendant hands Castwell an exquisite imitation, and Castwell begins to fish. In short order he lands a lovely two-and-a-half-pound trout.

Another, exactly like the first, rises in the very spot from which the first was taken, and the scenario repeats. Trout after two-and-a-half-pound trout is taken from the same spot, in the same way.

Castwell wants to move on to other trout. The attendant forbids it. Castwell wants to stop fishing. The attendant forbids that, too.

There is no change—in time of day, in weather, in the look or feel of the trout, in the sequence of the battle. What had once been refreshing recreation becomes drudgery.

I can say it no better than Skues's characters:

"Hell!" said Mr. Castwell.

"Yes," said his keeper.

There are few pleasures to equal the taking of large trout on small flies, but nothing remains pleasurable forever. Without variety, even the challenge of big fish on minuscule imitations begins to lose its attraction, and that, fortunately, is when the big bugs appear.

Every great river has a big-fly hatch that anglers anticipate with great eagerness. Throughout the West, *Pteronarcys califomica*—the salmonfly, the giant black stone fly—attracts great interest. Large fish that are seldom catchable, monsters that hold in the depths throughout the year, become greedy, foolish, rising without caution. Anglers chase the hatch as it moves upriver, taking large trout on dry flies, trout that were accessible only to weighted nymphs—if at all—before the stonefly emergence. Similar behavior in trout and anglers occurs with the appearance of *Hexagenia limbata*—the Great Olive-winged Drake, Michigan Caddis, Fishfly—in the northern Midwest, and *Ephemera guttulata*—the Green Drake—of Eastern water. There are giant caddis that bring rivers to life, and on some streams intense surface feeding is caused by the hot winds of summer and the appearance of grasshoppers struggling on the surface.

The San Juan has such a hatch, but it is not widely known and the reason is simple: like the legendary Michigan Caddis, a hatch that seems to be more famous for the regularity with which it is missed by anglers than the actual fishing it produces, the big hatch on the San Juan is virtually impossible to predict. The hatch about which I speak is the fall of carpenter ants that occurs annually.

I can hear a dozen San Juan experts guffawing in the background. Folk wisdom has generated any number of rules to predict the hatch.

"You fool," they snicker. "It's easy to guess the date. All you have to do is watch for a long dry period after a wet spring. If you're on the river the day after the first big rain, you'll hit a hatch of gigantic proportions. Or is that two days after the first big rain following a dry spell? Or maybe during the first week following the second big rain after the first long dry spell of summer?"

In my experience, the ant fall generally comes after a big rain, and because this river sits in a desert, that big rain usually follows a dry spell. But how long after which rain or dry spell, or where on the river it is likely to occur, I would be hard-pressed to guess. I have yet to anticipate the hatch, and many years I have missed it entirely, managing to be out of town for the day or week of its occurrence. Frequently it appears upstream or down from where I am fishing, and I find out about it only after it has passed. Sometimes, however, it materializes before me when I am on the river, and I luck into truly great fishing by accident.

There is little doubt when the hatch unfolds before you. It usually happens when the water is dotted with anglers happily fishing #26 midges on 8X leaders, patiently drifting carefully mended lines over fussy trout. Somewhere on the river a huge maw will inhale something from the surface. Then another fish will do the same. Sometimes it takes a few minutes for fishermen to catch on. Often the situation becomes clear only after you spot a pair of ants floating through the water. It is hard to miss the bug if one floats past you. Disheveled, huge, black—often floating securely fastened to the butt of another, like a couple of dogs still stuck together long after the heat has gone—mating pairs float by, sporadically at first, and then in profusion. The fish come to them as if they have never eaten. It is Thanksgiving Day at the rescue mission, cookie-package-from-home day at the university; it is manna falling on the desert after too many days of unleavened bread and midges.

The hatch is nearly impossible to fish incorrectly. A large, dark caddis or stone-fly imitation—a black stimulator about size #10 or a peacock caddis of the same size—works quite well. For years I tied a painstakingly exact spent-ant imitation with beautiful segments, legs, and diaphanous horizontal wings that caught fish but took far too much time to tie. The peacock caddis can be thrown together in a minute; it becomes more disheveled with every fish, and it seems to work even better (if such a difference can be detected in the fracas) after it begins to fall apart. Delicacy is unnecessary—3X and 4X tippet spools come out of deep pocket corners where they have been buried for months. The frenzy is upon us, and many a five-pound rainbow comes to the net with an ugly black dry fly hanging from the corner of its mouth.

My memories of the hatch are many, and strange. The worst day I ever spent on the river—on any river—occurred during the ant hatch. So did several of the best. It is a time of extremes. Most fishermen who have gained a measure of angling maturity will tell you that the deepest pleasures in angling come from days spent astream with good friends and difficult fish. Forget it. When the big bugs are on the water, such maudlin reminiscence vaporizes. There is much hootin' and hollerin'—a wonderful antidote to the introspection born of months of small flies, selectivity, and intense concentration. We become children again, as well we should.

But a bad day during this hatch is, likewise, far beyond average. It is not just bad, it is horrible. I had such a day several years ago, and I hope never to have another like it.

I appeared at the fly shop to find a middle-aged man, his thirteen-year-old daughter, and his fourteen-year-old nephew waiting for me. The man was an engineer from Phoenix—tall, brooding, serious. The daughter was short, overweight, her deep-set eyes ringed with dark circles. The boy was surly. What few words he spoke were snarled with a curled lip. There was anger in the air. And sadness.

As we drove to the river the man did all of the talking. I learned of his angling exploits: the famous people he had fished with all over the world, the sizes and numbers of fish taken on several big-name rivers. The daughter and nephew, I was told, had never been fly fishing before, and it was my job to get them started and to get them into fish. The engineer, I was assured, could take care of himself.

We began the fishing day with a dry-land casting lesson. The girl worked hard at it, and got it pretty quickly. The boy flung the rod around, oblivious to anything I said, obviously disturbed that his cousin was doing better than he was. The man—the boy's uncle—was anything but avuncular. He shouted advice to the boy, frequently contradicting my instructions. He didn't want to waste precious fishing time in the parking lot, so we left for the water.

I took them to a piece of open water where I expected few people, where there were no willows to snag a low backcast, where I hoped a few gullible fish might be willing to take deep, drifting nymphs before the hatch.

The man took fish immediately, and why not? He was over stupid trout in easy water with a pattern that had been taking such fish all week. I went there for the kids, fearing he would otherwise be disappointed. I had hoped to put him over some better fish in the afternoon, but it was clear from the first hookup that he hugely enjoyed these easy trout, this bland place; and he didn't seem to give a hoot about the kids. Every time he hooked up, he barked an order for me to come with the net; and each time he did so, I was pulled away from his daughter, who was in tears telling me about the bitter divorce that had given her to her mom for the school year, her father for the summer. It was a tragic story, and all of the agony of the experience was carried in her face. She was pouring her heart out, and I wanted to listen, but I was pulled away from her each time her tears began to flow by a fish-greedy father—or by her cousin who, having just created another bird's-nest tangle of lead, fly, and leader around his rod, would look at me with that snarl and yell, "Hey, guide, untangle me!"

On the way to lunch, we walked through Baetis Bend, where the ant hatch had materialized. Giddy fishermen were taking large trout on the surface with big, bushy, dry flies. There might have been a chance of squeezing three considerate anglers into the water, but not these three. I would have loved to give the joy of that experience to that sweet, sad girl, but my brain conjured images of a bragging father, a neglected daughter, and an undeserving boy. I made an executive decision: we left for lunch.

Separately, they made comments to me. The man wondered why I wasn't taking them into that water where the fishing seemed so good. The boy wondered whether we had to do this all day. The girl told me she never really wanted to go fishing, but she felt it was important to her father, and she hoped they might be able to "do some bonding."

At lunch Dad talked about all the fish he had caught. He never mentioned the ones he had broken off through ham-handedness. The boy complained bitterly about what a lousy time he was having. The girl listened to them both and quietly took a pill for her ulcer.

There is more, and I probably should save it for another time, but what the hell—as long as we're wallowing in misery, we may as well jump in with both feet.

I knew the hatch was building. I knew it might be the only day of the year that big fish would come up for big bugs. And I knew that by afternoon every fisherman on the river would know that the ants were on the water in the Lower Flats and Baetis Bend. Rather than add three more crazed fishermen to the frenzy, rather than destroy the experience for the few unfortunate enough to find themselves in our vicinity, I opted to fish the lower water, where there would be no ants and no crowd.

And, selfishly, wanting a chance to talk to the girl, I decided to fish where I would be able to ask the man to get out of his own needs for a few minutes and think about someone else. I took them to more good nymphing water—water where they would have a good chance to take some of the brightest, fastest, strongest fish in the river. I took them to a heavy run below Simon Canyon, above the Holy Water. I told the man that I would help his daughter in the heavy water if he would help his nephew.

And I warned him, "Keep an eye on the boy or he'll wander off into current he can't handle and drown!" He agreed.

I put the guys over fish, rigged their rods, and walked a hundred yards upstream with the girl. We made perfunctory casts over nymphing trout while she told me that her father hated his job, hated his boss, hated her mother for leaving him, and probably hated her as well. She cried bitterly, knowing there was nothing she could do to fix it. I wanted to tell her that she wasn't the one who broke it, and that she wasn't the one who was supposed to fix it. She never spoke of her own pain. She spoke only of her parents and how badly she wished she could make things better. I wanted to hold her. To tell her that she was a wonderful person, in spite of the messages she was getting from her father, that someday she would be grown up and able to seize her own happiness and destiny, and that her concern for others (God knows where she learned it) would bring her friends, and lovers, and happiness. But I never got to tell her anything. Before I could, I glanced upstream to see how the boys were making out, and I saw the man fishing away, oblivious to the fact that his nephew was wandering ever deeper into a fast, treacherous run. I sat the girl on the bank, raced upriver, and got to the kid just in time to grab him as he lost his footing, went in over his head, and began to float downriver to Farmington. He was shivering and blue by the time we got to the bank. As far as I was concerned, the day was over.

Somewhere, upriver, happy anglers were struggling to hold on to heavy trout that had taken bushy dry flies and run away, dancing on the water as they fled.

This is a hatch of extremes.

Choosing a single day to select as my best ever on the San Juan would be impossible. Days there have been good for so many different reasons—big fish, lots of fish, a difficult trout taken, extraordinary weather that emphatically revealed the power of nature, memorable times shared with friends—the list is endless. But there is no doubt in my mind that this day was the worst on this or any other river.

This tale of woe cries out for balance, symmetry and, quite frankly, something a little more pleasant. Its antidote is found in another day, one of the great ones, during the time of the ant hatch.

What better place to find the remedy for such mean-spiritedness, selfishness, sadness, and pain than in a church, and not just any church but the small brown adobe church that rests on the hill that overlooks the main parking lot and the Texas Hole?

I don't have much to do with organized religion. I'd like to say that my choice is due primarily to thoughtful reasoning and a well-articulated antipathy—and there may be an element of that. But the dominant reason I do not belong to a religious community or attend regular worship is simple: religious services have almost always bored me to tears. What little illumination and solace I have received from such things I have found in the mystery of liturgy, in the sound of hymns echoing from the high spaces of Gothic cathedrals, in the drone of languages I could not understand murmured in dark sanctuaries penetrated by shafts of sunlight through stained-glass windows. But even liturgy, song, and sacred architecture begin to lose their power with familiarity. More often than not my experience of organized worship is one of fidgeting, of struggling desperately not to fall asleep, of wondering more about when it would be over than about the nature of my relationship to a Divine Being. I wish it were otherwise, but it is not. I have always found more meaning in nature, more illumination in the glow of sunrise than the incandescent light of indoor worship. There is more than enough sublimity in watching the sun set from the shore of a high mountain lake, as alpenglow colors the towering peaks crimson and a chill descends, bringing a shiver; more than enough mystery and mysticism in the beauty and enormity of the night sky—pinpoints of unfathomably distant white against a black background of nothingness; more than enough meaning to be gleaned in the complex tangle of matter and life, the interrelationships that are contained within a single cubic meter of forest floor. I have found solace in the sound and feel of water running over rocks—the dazzling reflection of sunlight off and through droplets thrown into the air in the collision of gravity-pulled water with earth-rooted stone, the white-noise roar, the constant yet complex buffeting tug of turbulent water on my legs. I have been alone with my thoughts and my prayers, beneath high trees that passed brilliant shafts of light into the darkness of the dense forest, and I have rejoiced in the golden, dappled glow of an autumn aspen glade. So it is no surprise that I did not go into the adobe church that day a few years back but waited outside, instead, preparing lunch for Ron and Chris, who had gone to worship.

Ron and Chris are brothers-in-law and good friends. They often fish together, and do so with great seriousness and intensity. Which is not to say that either of them is a drudge. Quite the contrary, jokes and stories fly about in their company, but always, at bottom, they are there for the fishing. As is often the case with friends who fish together, there is rivalry. This, too, is good-natured, but no less serious than their love of fishing.

If I were to enter the world of their rivalry as referee and judge, I would have to call the morning a draw. We had fished a back channel full of midging trout, and even though there were ants on the water, it was a difficult choice whether to fish the peacock caddis or the midge emerger. Both produced excellent fishing.

Earlier in the week I had shown Chris and Ron how to fish the induced take with the midge, and both of them had become quite proficient. It was one of those delightful times on the river, a river where selective feeding is the norm, when large trout would take either a midge or an ant. Big fish were feeding in the shallows and could be hooked with a midge that had risen up into the film from a dead drift by throwing a straight-line mend and then allowing the line to tighten. Trout would also come up to eat the ant imitation drifting with the current, or twitched with the rod tip. It was a wonderful dilemma, and one that was resolved simply: we fished both bugs, and we hooked a lot of fish.

As noon approached we left the river for the church. Ron and Chris are devout Catholics who try very hard never to miss mass. I had driven by the church countless times over the years, but I had never driven the short road to its door. I wondered who would be there. I thought that it might be a group of visiting fishermen praying for better luck and was surprised to discover that the place was full of local people who called the church their own.

It was mere coincidence that found it on the banks of one of the world's great trout rivers. Workingmen, businessmen, farmers, and ranchers were there. Most were Hispanic. The welcome they extended to Ron and Chris was heartwarming. They walked by the tailgate where I was waiting and greeted me warmly, welcoming me to their community and inviting me to attend mass with them. I declined. Their friendliness was genuine, and I was reminded of the warmth I have often felt in the company of rural people, and especially in the company of Hispanic people who have lived in a place long enough to develop a strong sense of community, history, and roots.

A debate rages in states that have large Spanish-speaking populations about the merits of assimilation and the use of Spanish. Some have tried to pass "English Only" laws that eliminate spoken Spanish from the schools and from official forms. When I have heard speakers address this subject, those who favor assimilation and "English Only"—even those who are of Hispanic descent—usually speak with reference to recent immigrants. They talk about the need to leave behind the ways and language of the old country in order to learn the ways and language of a new home. This, we are told, will ensure prosperity. The discussion avoids mention of people like those who came to the church by the San Juan River, people whose history elsewhere is quite distant. The Spanish who settled New Mexico did so before the colonial outposts of New England were established. With the exception of the aboriginal people of the West, these Spanish-speaking people have the greatest claim to the title indigenous. They have broken this sandy soil for hundreds of years. What an insult it is to ask them to abandon their language in order to become part of a culture that is relatively recent, and in many ways inferior to the one they have established in this place.

I once watched Linda Chavez perform. Linda is one of the most vehement proponents of "English Only," an apologist who is sent around the country by a Washington-based conservative think tank to argue for the assimilation of Spanish-speaking people into the consumer culture. I watched as she dismissed the pain and sincere feelings of a Hispanic man who had come to hear her speak. He rose from the audience to speak to her about the bitter indignity and stinging insult he felt when he first went to an English-only school in the San Luis Valley, from the security and acceptance of his Spanish-speaking home. He spoke with great feeling of the embarrassment and humiliation he and others felt in that place. Linda Chavez stared him coldly in the eye and said simply, "You are better off for that."

She had no idea to whom she was speaking, and I imagine she could not have cared less. She was on a mission whose etiology I can only guess. But I do not have to guess about the man to whom she spoke so coldly and glibly. It was Reyes Garcia, who grew up tending ditches and working the family farm near Antonito. Reyes Garcia, who recently completed a year on fellowship at the Huntington Library in Pasadena. Reyes Garcia who teaches philosophy at the college in Durango. Reyes Garcia who is as intelligent and perceptive a man as I have ever known, a man who might easily have moved into the rarefied atmosphere of academic scholarship by forgetting his roots. Instead, he chose to embrace them. He could not forget them; they are too deep. He is held by powerful bonds of land, family, and community, and they refuse to release him into something less.

I thought about Reyes and the things he had told me about his people and his home that afternoon as I waited on the tailgate of my car. I had been fishing on the land of these people for years without ever acknowledging it until that morning in the red-dirt parking lot of the little adobe church, the church where I was greeted with such friendship and warmth.

Ron and Chris emerged ready for lunch, and ready to fish. We returned to the river with peacock caddis on our leaders. The trout came willingly, but more willingly to Chris's flies. He took fish with nearly every cast. Good-natured kidding was followed by laughter as the tally grew ever higher in his favor. Ron insisted that Chris's thoughts must have been impure during mass. I wondered if, perhaps, Chris had prayed for victory while Ron had prayed for something more noble. I know that it doesn't matter, and that I will never know what their thoughts had been as they prayed. But I do know this: these guys truly loved each other, and it was wonderful to fish in their company.

That afternoon in a place I newly understood as one of history and community, the home of kind and gracious people, a place where I was a guest, the ants were hatching, the fish were eating, and it was our turn to be the happy anglers.

It was our turn to try to hold onto heavy trout that had taken bushy dry flies and run away, dancing on the water as they fled—our turn to savor the moment, our turn to experience the great joy of this hatch of extremes.

HOLY WATER

THE ANTS ARE UNPREDICTABLE; they never last very long. Soon after their sudden appearance they disappear just as suddenly, and the fish, for the most part, go back to eating midges.

Throughout the year there are exceptions to the small-fly rule. Baetis show themselves sporadically, peaking in the fall months, but they, too, are often small. Olive stoneflies, about a size #16, appear infrequently in early summer—some years not showing up at all. Caddis sometimes make dusk a time of furious activity in July and August. Good-sized hoppers and crickets bound from the grass into brush-lined back channels, and a deer-hair imitation of either will often take bank-hugging trout in the warm months.

In July and August a respectably large mayfly appears: *Ephemerella infrequens,* the Pale Morning Dun. Although it hatches more heavily in some years than in others, the hatch rarely fails to occur, and its timing is almost like clockwork. PMDs begin to show in the middle of July, hatching in greater and greater numbers on into the first weeks of August, after which their numbers dwindle. Typically the dun is a size #16, yellow-bodied, with transparent wings that sparkle in the harsh overhead light of summer. On the

San Juan those diaphanous wings shine even more brightly than they do elsewhere because the PMDs appear on the Holy Water.

Between the powerful currents of Simon Canyon and the heavily fished runs of the catch-and-kill bait-fishing water that flows beneath the large cottonwoods of the state-park campground, there is a broad flat that is like none other on the river. For most of the year it seems empty, devoid of fish and fishermen. Few anglers risk a trek into this water, and with good reason. Although some of the most beautiful trout in the river live there, they are difficult to find. The hatches that would bring trout into the shallows—the profuse sheets of insects that would give them reason to risk taking positions where they can be seen by predators—do not often occur, and while a hatch of midges or *Baetis* might take place, causing a few fish to surface on any given day, although evening caddis might flutter across the water bringing slashing rises to naturals and skating, hair-wing imitations alike, more likely the fisherman will sit on the bank, waiting, as the sun gradually sinks behind the sandstone mesas—as the afternoon and evening end, fishless.

This beautiful water is a place the drift boats float through on the way to Last Chance Riffle and the boat ramp, a lovely, quiet place of reflection and the occasional fish or two before hauling the boat onto the trailer and heading in at the end of the day.

So why the honorific title? Why the glorious name?

Perhaps it is the setting.

The Holy Water is best viewed from above, from the top of the sandstone cliff that sits slightly upriver. From this viewpoint, the Holy Water shines in late afternoon, catching the light of the descending sun, breaking it into myriad reflections, and giving it back as a ribbon of liquid diamonds. Downriver the water takes a hard left and breaks into braids before coming together again in the dark-trunked forest of old riparian cottonwood. In winter these trees are twisted, gnarled, and black—leafless, but in the spring and summer they shimmer and shine like the water, their green leaves catching both the wind and the light. In autumn, the golden cottonwoods that are the background in this view of the Holy Water are without equal on the river.

Behind the cottonwood, red and tan sandstone bluffs and buttes retreat, becoming more and more hazy, less and less distinct, until the faint blue horizon and a hint of Arizona mountains meet the broad expanse of the Western sky.

The water is gentle here. It moves slowly, if steadily, ankle to knee deep throughout the summer. In the high flows of spring, the current is swift and treacherous to wade, but it is fished by wading anglers so seldom at high water that few, if any, think of the Holy Water as anything other than a beautiful shallow flat. Its clear, transparent water flows above a bottom of fist-sized multicolored rocks, gravel, and an occasional large boulder. It is water that is waded easily, full of fish that are rarely seen and more rarely caught— fish that are as wild, colorful, and full of fight as any on the river.

That is, until the PMDs appear. The fish are still wild and colorful, often a bit more orange on their flanks than their silver-sided brethren upriver, but they are no longer invisible. When the PMDs cover the Holy Water on an August afternoon, the flat fills with dimpling trout, trout holding in a few feet of water, large, visible trout that sip gently and steadily—trout that are susceptible to a yellow Comparadun or Sparkle Dun, a Harrop CDC Transition Dun, a quill wing no-hackle, a Lolita (more on this later), or maybe a well-presented Light Cahill tied thorax style.

~

There are few buildings along the river now that most of the land beside the regulated water has become state park. A dilapidated and abandoned tackle store slouches into ever-deeper disrepair along the highway near the turnoff for the road that goes to the lower boat ramp. There is the small Catholic church that sits beside the entry to the main parking lot near the Texas Hole. The Bureau of Reclamation has a few buildings and some chain-link fence up near the dam, but for the most part, the riverside has been left alone. The cliffs rise and fall. Side canyons enter through riparian niches full of willow and occasional cottonwood. Trails wind through rabbitbrush, tumbleweed, and sage. There is little asphalt to be endured, few fences to negotiate, and hardly any man-made structures. Above the Holy Water, occupying the high bluff toward which the river reflects its diamonds in the late-afternoon sun, there is a house trailer behind a small fly shop. The trailer was once the home of Joe and Diane Kresl. Recently, Joe and Diane moved downriver a short distance to a new home, but I will always associate that trailer, that spot, that wonderful view, with them.

Joe began fly fishing when he was eight on the rivers of the front range in northern Colorado: the Platte, the Poudre. His father got him started, but his passion carried him beyond childhood experience into the somewhat rarefied atmosphere of the truly gifted angler. Anyone who has seen Joe cast knows what I mean. His motion is economical. Line rolls off the tip of his rod without a ripple. Clean, tight loops carry a fly along for the ride, delivering it with accuracy and delicacy at distances that find most anglers straining, pushing too hard. Anyone who has watched Joe fish, watched his predatory intensity, watched him select a rising trout, seen him cast with precision, strike with certainty, quickly play and land fish, anyone who has watched a trout resting in his sure hands waiting for release, knows that Joe's abilities as an angler transcend those of most fishermen.

Joe is a guide and fly tier. He has tied thousands of dozens of flies and reached the point where each one that he ties carries his imprint: the idiosyncrasies of fly-tying style that allow anglers without his talent to take fish. I carry Joe's Thorax Adams in my box at all times, and whatever other flies he might throw at me when I see him.

"Hey, Steve, take this and let me know if it catches anything."

It always does.

I fish with Joe whenever I can—which is not often enough—because he is a fine angler, a fine and thoughtful person, and because there are few whose company I enjoy as much.

A few years ago, Joe and I shared an afternoon on the Holy Water. That afternoon has grown in retrospect until it is no longer just the memory of a day on the river. The day—filled with violent weather and rising trout, with sheets of PMDs that covered the surface of the wind-crusted water, with the remembered image of Joe's intense, hunched figure rolling out slender loops of line through the dark sky—has become metaphor.

Although we get to fish together far too little, Joe and I spend a great deal of time talking. We talk each morning at the shop, while waiting for our clients to arrive, as we step into waders that too often are still damp from the previous day's guiding. We speak when we meet on the river and again in the evening as car doors slam and clients drive back to their motel rooms or home. Sometimes we talk into the evening—long after we have left the river, long after our gear has been taken down and put away, long after the need to speak about fishing has left us and the need to measure the scope of a broader context has seized us.

Joe is a religious man. I don't want to imply that he is one of the many small-minded people who make you nervous with their faith, people who hurl religion like a stone at the unsuspecting, wounding the heathen with assaults of piety. He is never pushy. He is never condescending. He is a deeply devout person who enjoys speaking about his carefully reasoned and hard-won faith with those who share an interest in such things.

I fish with Joe, and I talk with Joe as a colleague and friend who comes at these matters of angling and of faith from a slightly different perspective than my own. My beliefs are less clearly defined than Joe's. The things that I do not know, the questions that haunt me, greatly outnumber the answers I have wrestled from experience. But my interest is no less intense. Although my angling is a bit less polished and my beliefs considerably less clear, it is not for lack of trying. Just as there were mentors in my angling life, so too there have been wonderful people who shaped my thoughts on deeper matters.

My neighbor when I was a small child was a rabbi, Howard Singer, who wrote a novel that did pretty well (*Wake Me When It's Over*)—a novel that subsequently was made into a movie, providing him with the means to leave his work in a local synagogue in order to pursue writing full-time. I remember hours of conversation with him, and the hundreds of questions that I asked and he answered patiently. Later, as a college undergraduate,

I found that my best friend was a Lutheran—soon to be Episcopal—New Oxford theologian of the first rank, Robert Webber, a professor who hired me to paint his house so that I could raise the money to take every course he taught (at one point he helped pay my summer-school tuition so that I could continue to study with him). Through him and others I discovered the richness of the contemplative and mystical traditions in Western theology, the power of liturgy, and the significance of sacred architecture. I was trained in the traditions and content of formal theology: doctrine, apologetics, and hermeneutics. More important, by temperament I enjoyed the pursuit of such studies, even when they yielded no clear answers. I have long since abandoned the formal study of such things and any formal faith as well, but this is some of the intellectual baggage that I carried with me to the Holy Water that stormy day.

Trout were rising to Pale Morning Duns. The shallow flat was covered with rings when the wind was not blowing, but thunder rumbled in the distance, and rain came in heavy squalls, pocking the water when it did. PMDs littered the water, and trout fed steadily even through the blows.

Joe and I took positions about forty feet apart, casting toward each other into the pod of fish that were rising between us. We continued the conversation begun on the walk from the trailer, down the cliff to the stream. We spoke of faith and the gleaning of knowledge from historical texts. I insisted, as I always do, that I found the creation itself to be infinitely more revealing and accessible than written canon.

We agreed. We disagreed. We interrupted our conversation regularly to strike and play fish that had risen to our yellow artificials—smiling in pleasure each time one of us hooked up, grinning broadly when those beautiful trout ran, so full of life.

~

Every now and then, between bursts of conversation and fish—as we stood in the shallow flat watching the shadow form of trout in the murky currents of water made Cimmerian by storm—the sky itself would explode and we would shake with its rumbling.

Rose-sided visions would appear and disappear, rising from the dark depths momentarily, then sinking back into oblivion before their true measure could be taken.

~

Occasionally we would hold one of those apparitions in our hands for a brief moment before returning it to the unfathomable richness and complexity of the river from which it had been borrowed.

CARPE DIEM

COLD-WATER CONSERVATIONISTS have a passion for the preservation of native species. I applaud it. The fish-culture madness that seized American fisheries biologists in the late 1800s, and continues unabated in some states to this day, resulted in the genetic corruption or the outright destruction of far too many native populations. Whatever can be done to save the few remaining native fish must be done, and done quickly. But for many of the historic varieties of trout and salmon—varieties that developed singular behaviors and specific genes under the influence of the unique conditions that existed in hundreds of different watersheds and streams—it is too late.

Habitat is the primary need of trout, and much of their native range has been perverted far beyond the ability to sustain natives. What few native trout have not lost their rivers and streams to civilization have largely lost their identity to transplanted and hatchery-reared fish with alien pedigrees. In the Rocky Mountain West, the primary losers were the many varieties of cutthroat.

Historical accounts of stocking programs in the West indicate that the stocking that occurred here was simply the continuation of a pattern that had originated with the settling of the East. As soon as a region was populated with settlers, its rivers were either polluted to the point where they could no longer sustain native salmonids, or native fish were killed with such reckless abandon that artificial means had to be instituted to replenish fisheries.

The first restocking programs were anything but scientific and often were undertaken by sportsmen who simply wanted to see whether a favorite species could survive in new waters. It was not long, however, before state and federal agencies took over, expanding stocking programs to incredible dimensions. Brook trout were transplanted from Eastern rivers. Rainbow trout were brought in from the Pacific Coast. Brown trout that had been transplanted from Europe into the degraded watersheds of the East were also introduced into Western waters. Hatcheries were built and the genetic material of hatchery fish—material that had been evolving through millennia to satisfy the needs of trout in a distant drainage or more recently to ensure survival in the bizarre environment of the hatchery itself—was broadcast over thousands of square miles of mountain streams in the form of hatchery-reared fingerlings and "legal catchables."

Genetic science was in its infancy; so, too, was salmonid biology. We knew virtually nothing about the destructive consequences of transplanting and hatchery programs. Suffering the ravages of siltation and the higher water temperatures of indiscriminate, rapid logging, tortured by the consequences of human overpopulation and industrialization, losing their highly specific genetic identity through cross-breeding and replacement by introduced species, and through it all continuing to suffer the ravages of unlimited catching and killing, many of the varieties of trout that once swam in the isolated drainages of the West have ceased to be. Most of the Western cutthroat are gone forever, and there is nothing that can be done to save them.

~

Trout fishermen are aware of the transplanting and hatchery stockings that have destroyed native populations of trout, salmon, and char, and we are beginning to do what we can to reverse the trend; but we haven't spoken much about the warm-water fisheries that suffered much the same fate. The same fondness that anglers have for salmonids, they also have for other game fish. In the same way that favorite trout species were placed in nonnative waters, bass, pike, perch, various catfish, and dozens of other warm-water species were put into rivers, lakes, and ponds where they had not lived before—by well-meaning sportsmen and by government agencies.

Amateur fish culturists harbor a special fondness for decorative fish like carp and goldfish, and these fish are probably the pet fish with the longest continuous histories. Like the trout, they followed the movement of settlers and civilization. Native to Asia, they were introduced into Europe from the Near East. The carp was brought to America in the 1870s—the same time when nonnative trout were first being stocked in the West—and were soon introduced into Western water.

Few people travel to a distant river to fish for carp. Perhaps they are too common. Perhaps the places where they are found are too often ugly. Carp survive in some of the most overused, polluted rivers of the world. The sky above carp water is frequently gray or brown. The banks are often littered with old tires and the rusting carcasses of abandoned automobiles, refrigerators, and shopping carts. The backdrop is sometimes urban. But carp and carp-like creatures have been around for millennia, and their world has not always been so ugly.

Carp were domesticated in the Old World centuries ago: kept as pets, stocked as decorative additions to carefully tended ponds. They were not considered trash. The history of their introduction into the San Juan River is difficult to determine, but records of their appearance in the vicinity indicate that they were put into area waters both by government agencies and by private individuals. Records of their appearance in neighboring LaPlata County, Colorado, go back to 1872. Most likely, they escaped from private ponds into rivers and quickly established thriving communities. Like the trout, the carp of the lower San Juan River were introduced.

Carp flourish in the river, but they are not distributed widely in the quality water. Unlike another fish often found in trout streams and considered by some to be trash—the whitefish—carp are not salmonids, and because their needs are different, they occupy water that is shunned by trout. They are found in muddy backwater sloughs and in ponds that lack current when the river is lowered to its summer level. The water inhabited by carp is warmer, less oxygenated, less hospitable to trout than the clear, cold water of the flowing river.

Bud and I were seized by Carp Fever a few years back, and we spent many afternoons wading in muck that sucked at our boots when we tried to walk, creeping toward the places where carp could be seen only as ghostly shadows in the cattail-edged, brown-water ponds. Often we saw only the evidence of where they had been, the puff of smoke that is the disturbed sediment left behind when they are spooked—by wading anglers, by fly lines that land too harshly, by low-flying birds.

Carp-fishing technique is sometimes debated among aficionados, and although the literature of carp angling is scant, the oral tradition is not. Just as there is controversy among trout fishermen regarding ethics as it relates to tackle and technique, so, too, carp anglers debate the merits of the wet fly versus the dry, the dead drift versus the poacher's retrieve. You may suspect that I say this with my tongue in my cheek and, for the most part, I guess I do. It's not often you hear fly fishermen discussing the ethics of various carp-fishing techniques, but there are places where the trout fishing has become a circus and the discussion of carp-fishing styles offers a humorous and illuminating counterpoint to the sometimes-ridiculous foibles of trout fishermen. I have, in fact, heard carp technique debated hotly among the guides of the Bighorn, and I have debated it myself—always laughing under my breath—but laughing no more or less than I would during a similar discussion regarding trout. Self-righteousness and pious purism are common in our sport, but that doesn't make them any less silly.

There are some who argue, when the mood has seized them, that any carp taken on a submerged fly is taken unfairly, that the only carp truly caught is one hooked securely in the soft lips of a tiny, bottom-oriented, sucking mouth—stuck with the sharpened wire of a delicate dry fly. I feel otherwise. While carp frequently rise to midges on the San Juan, and I have even seen them go airborne trying to snare a dragonfly on the wing, such behavior is a violation of their nature. It is the behavior of foolish creatures, deviants. Carp that are true to their nature eat near the bottom. They are born to scour food from the bed of the pond, born to suck in detritus and bottom-dwelling vegetation, to ingest only an occasional macroinvertebrate. As the cutthroat is born to the gaudy, attractor dry fly, and the wily spring-creek brown to the perfect drab, dun imitation, the carp is born to the willowy wet fly, the Marabou Bugger.

I have been castigated for my methods by a few carp-angling, dry-fly purists, but I am proud and perhaps a bit stiff-necked in the face of criticism. Like G. E. M. Skues, who surrendered his rights on the chalk stream rather than knuckle under to the tyrannical Halford, I would rather be drummed off the best carp water on the river than cease to cast the noble Green Crystalflash Bugger. I refuse to watch a carp fly sitting daintily on the surface of the dirty water; I want to fish it, actively, with the deadly poacher's retrieve. Too many carp have succumbed to the method for me to believe it is anything but appropriate.

For those who are not familiar with the poacher's retrieve, I will describe it. The full subtlety of its application can hardly be communicated here, but enough of the method can be shared to facilitate something of a beginning—an ardent carp angler can easily spend (waste?) a lifetime discovering the nuances of the technique. Simply stated, it is this: the line is cast over promising water; an appropriate fly, weighted so that it will find equilibrium with its point riding up, is allowed to sink to the bottom. The angler waits, sometimes counting—to a hundred, or two hundred—long enough for the carp to forget about the cast, the angler, the intrusion. Then, a slow, painfully slow, hand-twist retrieve is effected, which causes the fly to wriggle, ever so enticingly, along the bottom. When a feeding carp is tantalized into eating the morsel, a deliberate, quick, yet gentle strike—so as not to rip the fly free of the delicate lips—is made, and the fight is on.

No trout, except possibly a very old, very heavy, very wise trout, fights like a large carp. At first it feels like deadweight. Then the weight begins to move—slowly, inexorably—away. Landing a determined carp is a bit like trying to hold onto the car you parked on a slight hill, the car you parked forgetting to set the brake. At first there doesn't appear to be anything wrong, but you sense something—perhaps a slight, barely perceptible motion. As the car begins to creep downhill, you grab the rear bumper, hoping to hold it against gravity and the gathering speed. But the hill is steeper than you thought, and the car so much heavier than you imagined it could be. Finally you realize that human strength has finite limitations. You cling to the car, never knowing until the last moment whether it will stop of its own accord or drag you wherever it wishes. So it is with a hooked carp if it is large. The carp does what it will. If you are lucky, it will stop moving, and you may even enjoy the illusion that you had something to do with it. Sometimes, after several such illusory moments, a carp will come to hand. Brilliant golden fan-like scales of enormous size will dazzle kaleidoscopically in the sun. Large, wise eyes and pouting lips will ask for mercy, and you will comply gladly.

Rudolfo Anaya is a Southwestern novelist of well-deserved stature. His writing perfectly captures and describes the roots of the Hispanic New Mexican people in the contradictory liturgical certainty of Catholicism and the amorphous mystery that is a mountain people's animist paganism—the knowledge of the priest, the power of the *curandera*. Fishing for carp near the banks of the San Juan River, standing in the hot desert sun, knee deep in the muck of a backwater slough with a fly-caught cyprinid in my hands, staring into the knowing eye of a brilliantly illuminated golden carp, I cannot help remembering that the emblem of God in Anaya's best novel was a carp.

I find myself wondering, too, as I fish for carp on this trout river in the middle of a pikeminnow desert, about the meaning of the word *indigenous*.

~

The Spanish who came to New Mexico came for many reasons. Exploration of the New World was motivated by greed, by religious fervor, by fear. The

Inquisition was in full bloom, and many who would have died under its murderous piety flourished as escapees to the New World. No matter why they came—for gold, for glory, for land, to convert the pagans, or to practice forms of worship forbidden them in the dogmatic Spain of the sixteenth and seventeenth centuries—the Spanish settlers that colonized New Mexico put down roots. With the passage of centuries an introduced variety became native. They came to view themselves as indigenous, especially in the face of later conquests by northern Europeans whose first foothold in the New World was the cold, rocky soil of New England. They bitterly resented the wave of new immigrants, the hollow justification that was Manifest Destiny. But they had done as much in their time. They had come with slogans of their own, and they, too, had displaced an indigenous people, a flourishing culture.

Now we are all here—Anglo-Europeans, Hispanics, Native Americans—trying to live, sometimes with conflicting goals and methods, on the banks of this river in a region we call the San Juan Basin. It is too late to argue about who was here first. We are all here, now. We live together—sometimes uneasily.

The river flows through sandstone walls. The walls were carved in stone that was once mud at the bottom of an inland sea, a sea that was displaced by the mountains that began to rise when the earth heaved itself upward fifty million years ago. The stone has seen the passing of the sea, the coming and going of the glaciers to the north, the cutting of the canyon walls by meltwater. The canyon walls have witnessed the coming and going of many creatures. They have seen the coming of man, and they will watch him leave. In the shadow of a sandstone cliff, the term "indigenous" loses all meaning.

~

Lunker Lane is a place of powerful water. Except during spring, when the river spreads into the sloughs and ponds of the carp, nearly the entire flow of the broad Lower Flats is gathered into its narrow channel. A single tiny back channel diverts some water just upstream from the Lane, but it is slow and shallow and carries little of the river's volume. The majority of the river's flow is pushed tightly against the canyon wall by an island of willow. Flowing through a channel several hundred yards long and only seventy feet wide, the currents of Lunker Lane are strong and deep. Few fishermen walk the bluff side of the river here. It is a place where shy creatures sometimes make their homes.

The sandstone walls of the canyon have been broken by weather, by the seasonal and diurnal cycles of melt and freeze that lever the stone apart over time. Blocks of sandstone rest against the canyon walls and upon the sandy soil. A thick tangle of sage, willow, and piñon—the same tangle that makes hiking difficult—creates habitat for many animals. Rodents and lizards dwell in the crevices between the boulders. Great blue heron hide their nests in the brush. Coyotes hunt, sometimes surveying the area from the cliff top, then working their way slowly down into the canyon to feed.

One summer afternoon, returning to the car with clients after a good day in the Lower Flats, I spotted a coyote moving through the piñon on the other side of the river. It walked with purpose toward some goal we could not see. It walked without concern, ignoring obvious cover, not seeming to care whether or not it was seen.

I had watched coyotes hunt before—slinking from crevice to boulder, from boulder to juniper, from juniper to willow, from willow to sage . . . to pounce with a sudden vertical leap, all four legs springing at once, launching the creature straight into the air before landing suddenly and without warning on a terrified ground squirrel. The brazen act we witnessed from the other side of the river was a hunt, too, but definitely not a stalk. The coyote strolled as if with a swagger.

You can sometimes tell what a coyote is after by the way it moves. If it sneaks through cover, pausing, hiding behind stones and shrubs, it is most likely after a squirrel or some other rodent. If it marches deliberately, it is often after eggs.

We stopped walking, and waited to see what the coyote was after. A great blue heron we had not seen until the coyote arrived at the nest rose and shrieked a raucous, raspy screech at the coyote. The heron-mother attacked with wings, claws, and bill, but it was no use. The coyote buried its mouth, jaws snapping, teeth biting into the nest, and emerged from the melee no worse for the wear, its face glistening with the contents of broken eggs, its snout dripping the whites and yolks of what had been incipient life. The coyote strolled back up the cliff. The great bird flew off with slow, deep wing beats—upriver and out of sight.

One of the fishermen in the party, never having seen anything like it before, blurted out, "Wow, that was just like a Disney movie!"

Actual nature.

Although it is a tailwater, a place that we have to a very large extent created, the San Juan tailwater and other places like it are no less habitat, no less natural. We begin to think that such places were made for us, made especially for those of us who are fishermen, but such thoughts are foolish. There are others who claim the place as their own.

~

I have been involved in many a fight with water buffaloes over the years, and in particular with those who want to see the water of the nearby Dolores River below McPhee Reservoir—another extraordinary tailwater fishery—used for irrigation exclusively, even when it might mean death for the trout, for the river otter that were reintroduced when the dam was completed, for the riparian habitat that exists downstream from the dam— a dense, winding band of ancient cottonwood that no longer receives its necessary annual springtime flooding.

I remember one particularly heated exchange during a public meeting, an exchange during which the director of the Durango Bureau of Reclamation Project Office looked me right in the eye and said mockingly, "There was no fishery before we built the dam, and you guys fought the dam all the way, now you fight us about how we release water. Well which is it? What do you want? A natural river? An artificial fishery? I don't get it!"

Like a father who leaves town after the birth of an unplanned child, feeling no sense of responsibility because the child he created was unwanted, the bureau, historically, has felt no responsibility for fisheries, for habitat, for riparian ecosystems that came into being or were radically altered by the building and management of dams. Whether or not they want to accept responsibility for their fathering, they changed the habitat and allowed new life to come into being. They cannot be allowed to walk away from it.

There may be concrete at the head of the tailwater, but the carp don't mind. The coyote and the heron don't much care. The trout don't seem to know.

It is a uniquely modern dilemma. Our power to alter nature is immense; and at the same time, we, too, are natural. Prudence dictates caution. Our history of biological meddling reveals that we know too little about the complexity of the natural world to presume to manage it. And yet we cannot help changing it with every step, every breath that we take.

Native trout, we have learned, cannot be removed from their home water and transplanted elsewhere without setting into motion an often disastrous and entirely unpredictable chain of events. I lament the passing of native species through habitat destruction and foolish attempts at fisheries enhancement. I am deeply saddened by the history of the displacement and murder of indigenous peoples. I am appalled by war and injustice. The corner of my soul that carries the moral burden of my own hubris, my own ignorant actions, grows heavier each year. And yet, the long view, the geologic perspective, tells me that future glaciers will wipe the slate clean.

Nothing has helped me understand the complexity of this dilemma—its burden, its humor, its contradictions, my own release from its terror—like the uniquely, laughably absurd irony, the glorious pleasure, that is fishing for carp on this crowded, world-famous trout stream.

COMING OF AGE

THERE ARE FEW IMMUTABLES in this life but one thing is certain: all young parents will swear not to repeat the follies of their own parents—and will then proceed to do just that.

My father was a hunter and rifleman. I suspect the only time he was truly happy was when he was in the woods stalking game with a bolt-action Winchester Model 70 in his hands. Sighting-in a rifle at long range on a piece of wide-open land ran a close second. When he could do neither, he puttered with his guns—cleaning and lubricating, rubbing the deeply figured, checkered wood with rich-smelling linseed oil. As often as not, I was there beside him soaking in that smell—the smell of the woods, gunpowder, and oil.

He dabbled in shotguns and skeet, and occasionally fired a few rounds at paper with a .38 revolver, but the bolt-action rifle was his hobby and his love.

I began target shooting with rifles as soon as I was old enough to hold one for more than a few seconds without collapsing in fatigue. I don't recall ever being asked if I wanted to do it, it was a given. I remember spending an evening a week at the target range working my way through the NRA sequence, patiently adding all of those sharpshooter bars along the way. After gaining proficiency lying on my belly—my right leg drawn toward my chest in the modified-Estonian style made famous at Camp Perry—I added kneeling and offhand as the bars, patches, and medals accumulated.

When I went off to college, it was a natural thing for me to join the rifle team and continue to shoot in the International Match format—small-bore, three-position—I had been trained in by my father. The .22-caliber sporting rifles, and fixed-stock, heavy-barrel target rifles I had shot as a child were replaced with a surreal-looking Winchester 52 International Match model that had an adjustable butt with an underarm hook, a beautifully sculpted palm rest, and an anatomically shaped pistol grip with a thumb hole.

Somewhere in the middle of my freshman year, however, I realized that spending my afternoons in a dark, smelly, overheated target range, having to travel every Saturday to another equally oppressive place to compete, spending far too much time with the blood supply to my left arm shut off by a cuff sling (so there would be no pulse to disturb the sight picture) was not—and never had been—my idea of fun. Instead, I began to run around outside, reveling in sunlight and fresh air, kicking a spotted ball toward teammates and a netted goal. Soccer became my life. It was something my father had never done.

~

My son, Daniel, landed his first trout around the time of his fifth birthday. It was a stocked rainbow taken on a spinner from Molas Lake near Silverton, Colorado. His empathy for the fish was immediate, and with tears in his eyes and a thousand apologies, he released it. Swearing not to be like my own father, I never pressured Daniel to fish, but I wanted him to like fishing as much as I did.

He began casting a fly rod in the grass not too long after that first rainbow. Before long he was fishing Lime Creek beside me, but he never fished very long. The woods always appealed to him more than the fishing, and his time was spent among the aspen and in the dirt. Water was for skipping stones, for jumping into from high boulders, for splashing around in after I had fished my way through.

He accompanied me on many trips, but the pattern remained the same, even after he had grown into the kind of young maturity that gives focus and patience to a child, but only for the things he chooses to love. We traveled to Canada for salmon and steelhead. I would fish a pool beside him for a few minutes, but he would always lay the rod down to go off into the woods, or to begin the building of what he called "water projects": huge dams of river rock, holding back the flow of tributary rivulets and streamside eddies. As I would work my way upstream, Daniel would remain behind, covered with mud, lost in his own thoughts—thoughts that had little to do with steelhead.

~

Daniel came of age as a fisherman three years ago. It was a year when the rainbows of the San Juan were rising freely to midges in the back channels, a season when our favorite piece of water was often deserted and always full of visibly feeding trout. It was a season of invention at the tying vise, of small, sparsely tied, thread-body pupae and emergers, of tiny clumps, and individual adults down to size #28. (We would gladly have tied #30s and #32s if we had had a reliable supply of hooks.)

My son began to fish beside me, but far enough away to lay claim to his own water. He began to land fish—difficult fish—without coaching or help. He took large trout on tiny flies tied to flimsy leaders, and although there was little of the giddy happiness I had seen in the past—the dam-building frenzy and splashing laughter—there was a level of satisfaction that seemed distinctly more mature.

Daniel had been tying flies since he was nine, beginning as most young tiers do with woolly worms. But the inventiveness of youth soon found its way to the fly-tying vise, along with the love of color. Neon and fluorescent yarns dominated his creations. The colorfully dyed necks I had acquired for tying steelhead and salmon flies soon found their gaudy-orange, purple, green, red, and blue feathers plucked for trout flies. Flies that might best have been used as Christmas-tree ornaments, that might have been found dangling from the ears of green-haired masochists with safety pins stuck through their noses, were tied instead to gossamer tippets and paraded before startled brookies that had no choice but to eat them or go blind from the glare.

But this season a degree of patience unlike any I had seen before came over him. It appeared on the water first, and then at the tying vise. His first midge flies took him hours to produce, but soon he was quickly tying pupae as beautiful as any I have seen. Every now and then, a tiny dry fly, a work of art, would emerge from the vise in his hands. The inventiveness that had found him plucking the streamer-necks a few years before was now demonstrated in pattern modifications that mimicked the colors and behaviors of life.

He had become a fisherman.

The last day we fished together that summer, I sat and watched. He had no idea that I was not fishing, so intense was his concentration. He was working a slot of slow water that pressed up against the far bank, fifty feet away. Some good trout were feeding on the far side of a much faster current. Daniel rolled the slow, open loop that is characteristic of his style out toward those trout, gently landing an unweighted emerger a few feet upstream from the feeding fish. A good mend followed the cast, then a good drift, and in a half hour or so of such deliberate fishing, he struck, played, and landed three trout.

Pride is a wonderful and terrible thing. Pride makes you try to do things well, and it gives you the strength and confidence to act in difficult circumstances. But pride can also make you rest in past accomplishment or in the illusion of accomplishment; it can make you lazy and boastful. However, the parent who is without pride in his child is probably also without love. I have been so full of happiness and pride at times that I have been scarcely able to breathe, and that day was one such time.

We have fished together little since that day. Daniel has discovered other things. Tackle catalogs have left his room and in their place he has piled reams of bicycling magazines and parts catalogs. His heroes have names like Miguel Indurain and Daryl Price, not Ray Bergman and Roderick Haig-Brown. He still loves the woods and would rather, I think, spend a few days camped beside a river than anywhere else. The hiking and the woods are vastly more important than the fishing. Perhaps there will come a time a few years down the road when the rhythm of the fly rod and the vision of trout rising through the film to snatch artificials will grab his imagination once again. Perhaps not. But I have finally come to the point where I realize how little it matters. What matters, what remains, is the wonder, the freshness of spirit that has been Daniel's since the day he emerged from his mother's womb. What matters is the essence that is Daniel, and not whether he ever finds it necessary to express this essence, as I do, on a trout stream.

I, too, came of age that summer of tiny flies and large trout, that season of watching my son do so well those things that have come to matter so much to me—that summer, hopefully Daniel's last, of feeling he must be what I want him to be and not what he will choose to be on his own.

ON GUIDING

To these guides, infinitely more than to any transient sportsman,
the river is a living, sentient creature.

—Bliss Perry, *Revisiting a River*

I'M NOT SURE EXACTLY how I fell into it. It started with a lot of playtime on the river, and ended with most of my river days becoming work days. The details are sketchy and I feel more like someone who has awakened in a strange place not knowing exactly how he got there than a person who followed anything resembling a route or a plan. I know that guiding has deep roots in my temperament, but I also know that I needed a shove to get started. Thomas L. "Bud" Collins, III, gave me that shove.

Bud has worked a lot of strange jobs. He was a dishwasher for Jim and Elfriede Shane at the Goldminer's Daughter in Alta during the years he lived only to ski. He once worked as a ski-school director and ski instructor. He's been a professional musician—a drummer and mouth-harp player for various bands. At one time he made silver jewelry. It came out one day when we were talking about horses that he had worked as a cowboy up on the plateaus above the Grand Canyon north of Kingman, and that he'd been a rodeo cowboy—mostly a bronc rider. A few years ago we were driving through the San Luis Valley on our way to Montana to spend a few days fishing with Tom Montgomery, and I learned that he enjoyed a brief career of rescuing bronzed wood from the sides of abandoned barns for sale to the owners of fashionable bars in Aspen.

It was a time when weathered barnwood interior walls were the rage. We were just about to crest a hill on Highway 285, a small herd of pronghorn were running with the car about a thousand yards to the west, and Bud mentioned that we'd see a barn when we got to the top of the hill that kept him in chow one cold Aspen winter. Sure enough, when we crested the hill, there was a skeleton standing against the skyline, a decrepit old structure that was all frame and no walls. The walls had long since been removed by Bud and a couple of his colleagues in the barnwood business and were currently decorating a bar in Aspen.

That was the trip I suggested that he might think about working as a stand-up comic. Hell, what's one more career? We were rolling through Wyoming. The wind was blowing a gale and snow was traveling horizontally from west to east. The road was slick, and it was all I could do to control the car. The sign for the town of Rochester appeared. Bud turned to me with his head cocked off to one side (I would almost swear he was in blackface) and mumbled with a gravelly rasp, "Mistah Benny! Mistah Benny!"

I laughed so hard I nearly drove off the road.

During the time Bud and I were spending most of our days fishing together he chose to make his living as a fishing guide. He asked me if I was interested. I answered that I was. He mentioned the fact to Tom and John at Duranglers (folks I had known for some time) who were looking for another guide, and before I knew it people were paying me to take them fishing.

Guiding has taught me a great many things about rivers, and about myself. The most glaring revelation is one I have discovered only recently: it wasn't until I began guiding that my fishing stories began to have people in them, people like Floyd Ray and Jordan Green.

Floyd was one of the first to pay me to take him fishing. I met him at the shop on the river. He drove up in a dirty Ford Bronco with Arizona plates, and from the minute he opened the door, I liked him. He flashed me one of those wry smiles—the kind that comes a little bit more from one side of the mouth than the other—and I knew even though I'd never spent a minute with him, he was a character.

We talked a little as we rigged up, and I realized that this was also a man who didn't like to flap his gums for no reason. He was soft-spoken. He was quick with an answer when questioned about something, but he didn't volunteer a whole lot of information—at least not at this point.

I asked him where he had fished before, and he said, "Oh, I've fished some." I asked him what he did for a living, and he said, "I'm retired."

He said that he used to fish at Lee's Ferry a lot, but the fishing was off and he thought he might try the San Juan. For a retired guy with a dusty old Ford Bronco, he had some pretty nice tackle. That day he was fishing a four-piece Sage and a Ross reel. Whatever money he had for vehicles—and it didn't look like much—he seemed to have enough for good tackle.

We entered the river up high, near the dam, and waded downstream into the riffle about halfway between the dam and the cable that marks the end of the catch-and-release water. Immediately, he began to bang fish.

"Hey, this is pretty good," he said, and he flashed that smile again.

It continued like that all day. No matter where we went, Floyd banged fish. He took them from places where I had caught fish before. He took them from places I hadn't, and every now and then he took fish from places where I thought no one could take a fish. He was attentive to the ways of the river and he was willing to try things he hadn't done before if I suggested them.

He fished wet with a small yarn indicator. He fished nymphs by sight. He fished dries and emergers, flawlessly drifted over sipping trout. Everywhere we went that day, he caught trout. It wasn't that the fishing was easy—plenty of people we saw up and down the river were going fishless. I have never seen a person, man or woman, with such uncanny fish sense.

When we talked, we talked mosty about the river, about the insects, about the difference between feeding water and holding water, about the places trout were likely to be found on the San Juan. We talked about the fact that nymphs must almost always be fished absolutely drag-free and that this seemed much more important here than on many other rivers. Floyd finally opened up enough to allow as how he was seventy-one, retired from a job in the petroleum industry, and, gosh, he sure loved to fish. He said one thing I've heard said before, but never with such earnest, heartfelt sentiment. After landing the biggest fish of the day—a shiny rainbow trout of about five pounds, silver-sided and with small black pepper-like speckles, deep in the belly and as hard as a brick—I blurted out, "Jeez, Floyd, that's a gorgeous fish!"

Floyd looked me in the eye, still holding the heavy trout gently in the current with a hand around its wrist and another supporting its belly. His mouth drew back slowly into that lovely crooked smile, and he said, "Steve, they're all gorgeous."

I never threw a fly that day. I stood next to Floyd, making suggestions about where the fish might be, and what flies he should fish. I told him about trout I had seen before and what we might do to go about catching them. I watched him find fish I had not seen. It was one of the best days I've ever had on the stream.

Floyd has been a friend ever since. We fish together several times a year now, and in the interim I've learned a lot more about him.

At first I had him figured for a country boy. Few city boys I've known were as soft-spoken, spoke as little, or spoke words that contained as much meat when they finally managed to get their mouths moving. I imagined him working hard all his life, maybe as a farmhand or cowboy who turned to roughnecking for the good hourly wage before retiring. I guessed that he had saved his money carefully so he could spend some time fishing when he stopped working—saved enough to get a good rod and reel. I was only partly right.

The second time I fished with Floyd I realized that I had a lot to learn about him. He drove up in a shiny big Mercedes, popped out of the door with that infectious smile, and immediately apologized for the car.

"My wife is with me this time, Steve, and she likes this one better than the Bronco."

He went to the trunk and began rigging a different Sage, this time with an Abel reel.

He was born in Oklahoma and he'd worked hard all his life, but he didn't break soil, and he hadn't broken horses. He started out as a wild-catter—a guy who drilled for oil. He'd been as good an oilman as he was a fisherman.

Floyd is part geologist, a man with extraordinary knowledge of the ground and what's in it. I imagine he can look at dirt and know whether or not there is oil under it, the same way he seems to be able to look at water and know whether or not there's a fish in it. He is a petroleum engineer, a man who carries enough knowledge and authority to walk onto a drill rig and take charge. He is an entrepreneur, a risk taker. By the end of his career, he had founded, owned, and sold several small oil companies. He still likes to go sticking his nose into the ground to sniff out oil. (More than once, he interrupted our trip home after a day on the river so he could call a drill rig to see how a hole was going.)

Since that first day I've learned that he's fished from the Rockies to Alaska, in the Keys and the Caribbean, in Patagonia and New Zealand, in saltwater and in fresh. His good friend Victor, who joined us on a few trips, told me that Floyd once golfed well enough to consider turning pro. But he doesn't golf much anymore.

"It's kind of boring, Steve. I'd really rather fish."

These days when we go out, I carry a rod and fish alongside Floyd. I have always been comfortable with him, and I like to think that he's com-fortable with me. He still catches fish everywhere we go, and he still has that wonderful smile. Just a few days ago, I got a postcard from New Zealand with tales of big browns written on the back. I expect we'll go fishing when he returns.

When I try to understand the etiology of my transition from amateur to pro, from recreational fisherman to working guide, I always go back to a day fifteen years ago when I was on a high, exposed ridge with a group of inexperienced hikers and a climber friend. It was getting late. The sun had disappeared behind the nearby peaks, and a chill air had replaced the warmth of high-altitude sun. Our group was growing cold and tired, and I knew that we had to keep moving if we were going to get off the ridge and home safely before it became too dark to climb safely. We had come to a place where the route was terribly exposed—steep slopes fell hundreds of feet on both sides of our narrow perch, and we needed to make a delicate move into a narrow chimney in order to continue the descent. I felt responsible for the group because I had organized the hike. Without thinking much about it, I took some of the extra parkas I'd been carrying out of my pack and distributed them to those who were getting cold. I started to tell some incredibly stupid jokes.

"Does this bus go to Duluth? No, it goes beep-beep. My brother went to Alaska. Nome? Know'm? Of course, he's my brother."

While I was making a fool of myself, I put a harness on each hiker, tied them into the climbing rope, and one by one, belayed them down to a relatively flat spot where the descent became easier. We made it down without incident, without much difficulty, and I took a lot of abuse for my lousy jokes.

At the bottom, the other climber in the group—the woman who had taught me nearly everything I know about climbing—turned to me and said, "Has anyone ever told you that you've got the guide thing?"

The guide thing.

At the time I was not, and I certainly am not now, what you would call a great climber. But when I thought about what Dolores had said, I realized that she was right.

Long ago, when I lived in Denver, I spent a fair amount of time skiing in the Front Range with friends. Often I skied with my brother- and sister-in-law. David and Wanda had an Australian shepherd named Portia that was born to herd. When Portia came with us on a ski trip, she would cover miles running from the front of the group to the back, checking on everyone, saying hello—herding us up and down the trail. It was in her nature. The guide thing.

Years after that day on the mountain, years after Dolores's astute observation, I went to work as a guide. I have found it to be an occupation that suits me.

There are a great many people who can fish with extraordinary ability, and a few of these are professional guides. But it is not enough, by any means, to be technically competent. It is not enough to have fish sense. It is not even enough to be a patient and effective teacher. These skills have to be present to some degree, or a client is wasting his money; but not every competent angler can become a guide, and some of the best guides I know are capable but not extraordinary fishermen. It is temperament, not angling ability, that distinguishes true guides from other fishermen.

I know many guides. I know only a handful of really good guides. The best of them love to fish. They love to take people fishing. They assume responsibility for other people's safety and happiness as naturally and as competently as they button a shirt or pull on a pair of pants. But there is more. These are men and women who have spent enough time on a river, or a group of rivers, to know them as friends. They feel their presence as if the rivers themselves were thinking, feeling entities. Although such anthropomorphism is intellectually absurd, the feeling remains—having and needing no explanation. This kinship with the river is present in every great guide. And every great guide has a temperament that revels in the bringing together of friends: fishermen and rivers.

"Temperament, you've got that right!" I can hear a few scoffing. "I've been with dour ghillies in Britain who make you feel inferior the minute you step into the boat. I've heard them mumbling beneath their breath when I missed a strike or broke off a fish. Hell, it's practically a job requirement for them to be condescending."

From what I've heard, that's often true; however, a lot of old British traditions were challenged on American soil, and although the technical innovation that has taken place in North America is considerable, the disposition of the guides is no less significant a departure from the old ways. I am convinced for no good reason other than intuition, that the great riverkeepers and ghillies of Britain, men like Frank Sawyer, were no different from those of America. They knew and loved the rivers as friends, and they liked to take people fishing.

I met Jordan Green at the fly shop, and I knew right away that he was a city guy. Although he was soft-spoken, gracious, and gentle, there was an intensity beneath the surface that was palpable. He wore a pair of glasses thicker than any I have seen. His son Loren was with him.

Jordan told me that he was an attorney from Phoenix, and that Loren had just completed a degree in philosophy at Berkeley and that they were taking a break together before Loren had to leave for England. He was heading off to Cambridge to do graduate work. This was the first chance in years that they'd had to fish together.

Jordan had spent a great deal of time fishing the salt for tarpon and bonefish, and although he had spent a little time on trout streams, trout had not been his first love. Jordan's style had obviously been influenced by windswept flats and mangrove-lined, saltwater inlets. Every time he cast, he hauled. Lovely, tight loops rolled off his rod tip and carried his fly to distant water.

"Hey, Jordan?"

"Yes, Steve."

"That was a beautiful cast."

"Why, thank you."

"Just one thing."

"What's that?"

"It went over the heads of about twenty trout."

"Sorry, Steve, I'm used to tarpon."

We fished the Holy Water with copper-top nymphs and with yellow Sparkle Duns and we managed to land a few nice trout. The conversation never lagged, and it was rarely about fishing. Jordan's humor was the kind that festers in your mind, undetected for a few seconds—because of its complexity, because of its depth, because it is so dry it would make you pucker if you could taste it—and then explodes.

Loren spoke of Heidegger, in whom we shared a great mutual interest. He was going to Cambridge to study a branch of philosophy that has come to be known as Continental Philosophy to distinguish it from the starkly analytical approach of British and American philosophers, and Heidegger was one of this school's most influential thinkers. The significance and complexity of his work, the profound moral lapse that was his commitment to fascism and National Socialism, make the study of Heidegger a tremendously difficult intellectual and ethical enterprise. My dear friend Michael Zimmerman, a Heidegger scholar of considerable reputation, was going to be in Munich while Loren was at Cambridge and I suggested that Loren contact him if he traveled to Germany. The conversation went from Jordan's wonderful stories and dry humor, to politics, to philosophy. It flowed comfortably as the day passed. And every now and then, there was a trout to grab a fly and run with it.

I was testing a new fly that day: a half-nymph, half-dry fly tied on a long-shank hook. The rear half was the same as the abdomen of a pheasant-tail nymph, and it hung in the water beneath the surface. The front half was identical to a yellow Comparadun's dubbed thorax and fan-shaped, elk-hair wing. The elk hair and a little flotant held the front of the fly above the surface. I thought it might prove to be a good stuck-in-the-shuck emerger pattern.

In the middle of that hot August afternoon, a substantial trout that was taking emergers from the film grabbed the hybrid fly that Loren had been drifting through his feeding lane. The trout raced directly across the river, taking all of the line and about thirty yards of backing, then jumped high from the river, throwing a dazzling spray, when it reached the far bank. The fly came free. Of all the fish hooked that day, that is the one I remember most clearly: the gentle, confident take, the blistering run, the leap, the spray of water, the shimmering, airborne trout, and then the sudden vacant, loitering silence.

I took the fly off the tippet after we retrieved the line and handed it to Loren.

"Why don't you keep this one for a souvenir?"

"What's it called?"

"I don't know, Loren, I haven't named it."

"How about Lolita?"

"How's that?"

"Well, Steve, it's half-nymph, half-adult, and it's just about to ripen into sexual maturity."

Lolita it was, and still is. The fly continues to take fish from the Holy Water during the PMD hatch.

I have fished with Jordan a lot since that first day, and Loren has been able to join us on occasion. Jordan, like Floyd, has become a friend as well as a client.

He has learned not to throw a hundred feet of line if the fish are fifteen feet away. He can mend a delicate trout line in the air so that a nymph lands on the water ready to fish, a dry fly in position to take trout not having been dragged through the film and sunk by a long, late mend. Because his eyes are bad, every season I tie a few flies that I tie only for Jordan: spinners and duns with big puffs of polypropylene that stick up from the thorax, terrestrials with fluorescent orange tufts rising from their backs. He's an extraordinary caster and an experienced angler with a deep love of the sport, and it always saddens me a bit to think about how hard it is for him to see. But he is never sad and certainly needs no pity. He cherishes every day on the stream, without complaint, no matter the weather or the difficulty of the fishing. I've gotten used to yelling "Strike!" and bursting into laughter every time we hook (or miss) a trout.

We've spent days on small mountain streams, and on big rivers. Sometimes we drive my four-wheel into the mountains to see if there are any trout rising in a small lake. We've thrown streamers at cutthroats, hoppers at browns, and midges at rainbows. I've taught him a little about trout and he's taught me a great deal about tarpon, bonefish, snook, and permit, all species I've never seen but so dearly hope someday to experience. And he's taught me a great deal about life.

There have been many people I've fished with that I'll probably never see again. There seem to be more each year who come back as friends, as well as clients. They are as different as people can be. Some are wealthy; some are not. Some fish with great skill, and some have never touched a fly rod before. Some have fished all over the world, and some had only fished the streams near their homes before they made the journey to the San Juan, the Dolores, or the creeks of the San Juan Mountains. I find that it matters little how well or poorly a person fishes; what matters is the sort of person he is.

They come from the East and the West, the North and the South. Some come from overseas. They are city and country folk, men and women, young and old. The one common thread is the simple fact that I would never have had the pleasure of their company if I had not been guiding, and I would not have had the pleasure of sharing my rivers with them.

Some of this may sound simple, hokey, unsophisticated. I'm not a cynic. But I am not simple, nor have I led a sheltered life. I once held a woman in my arms, whom I loved more than anything in the world, held her and felt life ooze from her body as she shuddered and died. I've been rolled by junkies desperate for a fix, had my head smashed with a pipe, and felt hands go for my wallet even before I hit the ground, too dazed to defend myself. I have been in my share of fights with mean people, and I've fought back as hard and as dirty as I could. I've walked into explosions in strip mines and into rough bars, worked underground in open-stope gold mines. I have found myself by design or accident in enough bad situations that

I might easily be dead. But I'm not. Somehow I've learned enough to keep myself alive. I've known stupid, mean, spiteful people. I grew up in the city and I know urban life, with all of its uncertainty and agony. I am no stranger to angst. I lived twelve painfully and gloriously eventful years in a remote mountain mining community where people died by decapitation from mine timbers, from having their skulls crushed by falling rock, by electrocution from stray wires, and suffocation in bad underground air. I have struggled and watched others struggle to make a living. And I learned that when love and friendship, mountains and rivers brought us solace, none dared call it hokey. At least no one with any sense.

Few people could not compose a list of their own bitter experiences to justify cynicism, to put on the face of anguish and wear it proudly, hoping it might be mistaken for sophistication. But I am not a cynic. Cynicism is not a badge of honor and accomplishment, it is the response of the beaten—the sad face of defeat.

Why do I bring this up? Because the absence of cynicism is another of the requisites for a good guide.

Some guides fall victim to a superficial swagger. Most guides deliberately choose to live an isolated, sometimes difficult life, a life very different from the lives of most of their clients. Some think this makes them better than others. I have seen too many young guides mimicking the cynicism of an older guide in the misguided hope of acceptance and not as the result of their own experience. I have known bitter guides who resent clients for their wealth, for their angling inexperience, or for talking too much about what they have accomplished as fishermen. All of this strikes me as absurd. Wealth or its lack is never a measure of virtue, and I suspect that more than one guide has ridiculed a client's lifestyle more from insecurity about his own life than for any legitimate reason. Nobody I know likes to tell stories more than a guide; then why should we resent those of our clients? I find that I rather enjoy them. At the risk of revealing yet more of my sixties roots, I continue to believe that we are more alike—guides and clients—than different. We are all Bozos on this bus.

When a guide becomes bitter about life, he should find another job. If he should become resentful of the people he takes fishing, he should quit. When a guide gets burned out (as guides often do, as I often do toward the end of a long season), he should mark a few days off on the calendar to go fishing. When a client finds himself with a guide who belittles him, who would obviously rather be doing something else, he should find another guide.

It is not that there aren't bad days. It is not as if the people who would bother you somewhere else somehow fail to bother you on the river. A boor is a boor, whether on the stream or in town. But a guide has a job that should flow easily and naturally from his way of life, and that job is not just to help clients catch fish. It is not just to teach a few things about technique. It is not just to be a good companion on the stream. It is to share the wonder that comes from living in such close contact with a great river like the San Juan, to communicate the feelings and rewards, whatever they may be, that make him choose to rise early and go to bed late, to spend long days working in the wind and weather, to go home at the end of a long day to gear that needs attention, to a fly-tying bench that will see hours of labor before it can be left, and to a dirty cooler that requires cleaning and restocking, because he knows the river as a sentient being, and because he knows that he can help make people's lives just a little bit richer if they can learn to know it, too.

It is his job to share these things subtly, not in long speeches, to share them because he knows that it is every person's purpose to do more than just take up space on the planet—to find a life with meaning, and to live it— and that guiding, for now, is his way of doing it.

SOME UNORTHODOX ADVICE
REGARDING FLY RODS

AN OLD MAN FISHES the back channels of the San Juan. Beneath the brim of a small old white Stetson—more fedora than cowboy hat—is a weathered, brown face. Deep creases radiate from the corners of his eyes. His skinny frame is bent. He moves slowly, deliberately. When he ties flies to his leader, he tilts his head back so that he can peer at the tiny imitation and the hair-fine tippet through half-frame reading glasses that rest, far from his eyes, at the end of a large, drooping nose. His fingers, not as nimble as they once had been, tremble as he struggles to join the hook to the monofilament. The rod that is tucked beneath his left arm glows green in the late-afternoon sun.

It is a graphite Powell that was given to him by a dear friend many years ago. The grooved-foot reel that is fastened to the rod is a 3-inch Hardy Saint George as antiquated as the old man himself. It was already well worn when he acquired it at a yard sale, and he has been fishing it for fifty years. He wouldn't know for certain that he had a fish on if he couldn't hear its sweet purr. The fly was taken from one of the lidded compartments of an ancient Wheatley fly box. The brushed Silmalloy Metal box hasn't been made by Wheatley for years. Wheatleys will always be around, but the silver boxes of old have long since been replaced by nonglare black and anodized gray. He seemed to gaze at the box much longer than necessary, much longer than he needed to stare in order to select a fly. The box was given to him by his high-school sweetheart who passed away four decades ago, and he cannot remove it from his vest without thinking of her. There are better tools for fishing available than the ones he uses, or so he is told, but these are the things he takes to the stream, these are the implements he has come to associate with the San Juan River after a lifetime of fishing, and he'll be damned if he'll replace them just because some young whippersnapper tells him he should!

~

I have long had the involuntary and habitual compulsion to imagine the future. I wonder what the world will be like when my son is grown, what sort of person will he become? I wonder what kind of old coot I will become when old-cootness befalls me, as surely it must. At forty-five it might seem premature to wonder about such things, to imagine the future so vividly, but such is my temperament. Already, I am beginning to find answers to these questions, and they don't come just from my imaginings.

At seventeen my son has grown into the sort of person who delights in pointing out to his father what an opinionated old curmudgeon he is. I thought I was smack in the middle of middle age; instead, I am told that at forty-five I would have to live to be ninety in order to consider myself merely middle-aged. (Daniel thinks it unlikely that I will live that long, and now, raising a teenager, I am inclined to agree.)

"Face it, Dad," he says, "you're old!"

One of the things about aging that I like (and I'm happy to report that there is something to like, because so much of growing old is terribly distasteful—the failing memory, thinning hair, shortening breath, sagging pectoral muscles, expanding stomach, the aches and pains) is the fact that people expect you to be opinionated and narrow-minded. Even better, they excuse you these foibles and accept such otherwise unpleasant behavior out of respect for your years.

There are a great many things that I have very strong opinions about, and if typical conversation is any indicator, I'm not alone. One of the topics I can blabber about until the cows come home is fly rods: the look and feel of them, their actions, the materials they're made from, why I like some and hate others, and especially why I have come to dislike (much to my surprise, and in a total reversal of my earlier habits of conversation) any lengthy discussion of their mechanical specifications—such things as wall thickness, modulus of elasticity, resonant frequency, recovery rate, or tip deflection in millimeters per gram.

I don't often write dissertations about fly-fishing tools or accoutrements, and I imagine you can smell just such a treatise coming, but please indulge me. Although I am yet too young to have earned the right to anyone's gracious acceptance of my curmudgeonliness, I feel an uncontrollable desire to vent my feelings on the matter. Having peered into the future and also having had my suspicions confirmed by my all-too-honest child, I know that I will age without grace (apparently I have already begun to do so), and that I will become something of a crank. I thought I might get a little practice.

I do this in the absence of any other technical or gear-related tangents; and, after all, I am an essayist. An essayist, in case you hadn't noticed, is a person who—whether he wants to admit it or not—chooses this particular genre because he enjoys speaking about whatever he wants, with imperious authority, and without interruption.

The specious justification for this digression is that it will be an attempt to explain why I fish the rods that I do, and perhaps help someone else decide what rod he might like to fish on the San Juan if he hasn't already made up his mind. As you will shortly discover, this chapter really isn't going to provide much help along those lines, but it is my hope that more than a few readers will recognize their own views in this pregeriatric twaddle and enjoy one of the most important of the many pleasures associated with reading, which is: finding justification for one's own eccentricities in the words of another. The rest can buy a set of metric weights and go to the nearest fly shop to measure tip deflections.

I originally thought that I might title this chapter: "Some Unorthodox Advice Regarding Fly Rods for the San Juan River, a Little Zen, What Grecian Urns Have to Do with It, and Other Proof That I Am, in Fact, as Old as My Teenage Son Keeps Telling Me I Have Become," but I was afraid it wouldn't fit on the contents page.

For what it's worth, here's my sagacious advice:

Find a rod you like and fish it—a lot.

If I had any sense, that's where I'd leave it. As far as I'm concerned, these few words about sum it up. If the rod you use is no good and you fish it, you'll figure it out soon enough and swap it for another. If it's too stiff, too soft, too fast, too slow, too long, too short—whatever—you'll discover it on the stream. The only real test is fishing. The only useful test is you fishing—not some rod tester, and most definitely not some techno-geek who will presume to tell you that the only rod to get is the newest Purvis XLS XVIII Graphite with punctuated-modulus taper and helical-interdependent scrim, a resonant frequency of 2.31 seconds, and an average stiffness of 3.26 grams per inch.

Some rod makers create magic with their imaginations, with their hands, and others don't. Any of them—those who make magic and those who make garbage—can tell you why their rod is the best. All of them have graphs, charts, and measurements. Engineering may be one part of rod-making genius, but it is not the whole story. Science is necessary, perhaps, but it is definitely not sufficient.

"But I don't want to make a mistake," a youngster says. "Can't you give me better advice?"

Well, no, I can't, and as for worrying about making an expensive mistake—relax, everyone makes mistakes. What are you, a perfectionist? How many serious fishermen do you know who are still fishing the first (or even the second) fly rod they bought?

My opinions on fly rods are not naively antiscientific. When I was younger, I would banter technical minutiae with the best of them. I am not entirely unfamiliar with the technical component of rod design and manufacture, or ignorant of the mathematics and principles of basic engineering. It's just that temperament leads me to stress other aspects. This is why, sometime in the far-distant past, I went through a metamorphosis from freshman physics major to graduate student in studio art. This is why I no longer speak of modulus of elasticity. It is why I view with deep suspicion any fly fisherman who would rather talk about rod tapers than the fishing itself.

"But Steve," you protest, "how should a novice go about choosing a fly rod? How does he sort out the incredible variety of actions, designs, and materials?"

Again, the crusty old curmudgeon bellows, "Go fishing!"

Is there a best rod for the San Juan? A few years ago, I might have suggested a nine-foot, five-weight, fast-action graphite—something on the order of a Sage 590 RPL; or for those who like a somewhat softer, deeper flexing rod, perhaps a Winston IM6 in the same weight and length. I have fished and loved them both. Comparable rods by any number of manufacturers are made in this general category. A lot of San Juan anglers would have found themselves in general agreement with me—some preferring the extraordinarily fast Loomis or the slower Sage Light Lines. There are fanatical devotees of other labels: Powell, Scott, Thomas and Thomas, Orvis—to name a few. At the risk of offending the rod boutique aficionados, I have thrown any number of clients' Cabellas, Brownings, and Berkeleys, and more than a few no-name dime-store rods, with a significant measure of glee. Still, my general recommendation would have been a nine-foot, five-weight, best-quality, reasonably fast graphite rod you can afford.

That was before I watched Steve Cannon land trout after heavy trout on an Orvis one-weight, or spent a season fishing midges with a delightful seven-foot, nine-inch three-weight, Sage Light Line. It was before I decided that it might be nice to fish with my 5M-foot HDH, Cross Single-Built cane rod that had seen action only on small streams—in order to find out what it could do on bigger water. It was before I got an extraordinary four-weight Sage SP on a pro-deal (how can the average fisherman afford to buy one of these at retail?), and found what a joy it was with small flies and big fish. Finally, it was before I watched countless anglers successfully fish their favorite two-through seven-weight rods, some with extraordinary success, using a wide range of flies, leaders, and tippets.

This isn't very helpful, is it?

Where am I going with this? Precisely here: a case can be argued successfully for the use of many different rods, and the final judgment is not one of science. It is one of preference. It is one of angler temperament. It is one of art.

Which leads me into yet another digression, this one to dispel the notion that I am being antiscientific: Philosophy of Science recognizes that science itself is infinitely more complex than the commonly held view that it is simply a matter of gathering enough data to discover a pattern and then formulating a theory to explain the pattern. Even when scientists measure and quantify experience, accumulate data, and formulate an equation to relate the data (those of you who are nodding off, who already agree with me that this discussion is secondary—those of you with any sense—may skip this section and go directly to the stream), their final authority is not science, but art.

It has been demonstrated that for any set of data coordinates, in any coordinate system, there is an infinite number of equations that can successfully relate the data; the fundamental problem of science is choosing among them.

When I find myself before a group of students with a simple view of science, I illustrate this problem by putting a bunch of dots on a blackboard inside Cartesian coordinates, and drawing a series of absurdly complex, obscenely twisted lines through them all. The lines that reverse direction and go in circles are relations. The squiggles that go from one side of the blackboard to the other, bumping merrily along, up and down—without turning back to reconsider—are functions. All of the lines represent mathematically meaningful solutions. But when it comes down to choosing one of them, we choose it (if we are scientists), not because it explains the data with greater mathematical validity, we choose it because it explains the data more elegantly than the others. Because it is simple. Because it is beautiful.

Even for a scientist, truth is beauty.

Do you want to know how I finally settled on the few rods I now fish on the river? Through the years I have managed to acquire many fine fly rods. I've sold a few, given away a few, but thirteen remain—stacked in the corner of my office. I like them all and I fish them all, but I fish three of them far more than the rest: a nine-foot, three-piece, six-weight Winston IM6; a nine-foot, five-weight Sage RPL; and an 8½-foot five-weight Powell Western Sierra. I've had the Sage RPL for several years. I acquired the other two just this past season.

I'll deal with the Sage first: I fish it because it flat works. It throws a long line; it throws a short line. If I find myself in a gale with a five-weight, this is the rod I want in my hands. If I am forced to fish beneath the surface, to cast a lot of lead, to throw seventy feet of line, this rod will do it. If the wind dies and the trout begin to dimple the surface, it will turn over a long fine leader, and it will land a more delicate line on the water than any of the heavier rods I might have chosen to deal with the lead or the wind. It is, in a word, versatile. I don't love it. It seems too quick for love—more of a wham-bam-thank-you-ma'am kind of rod. I don't caress it. I fish it. But, as I said, it flat works and there are few trout fishing situations where it would leave me feeling either under- or overprepared.

Next, the Winston: I have been fishing Winstons, off and on, for several years. The shop I guide out of is a Winston dealer, and I have always considered it important for me to be familiar with the rods we sell. Over the

years I have fished just about every demo rod in the shop, but my favorite
has always been the six-weight Winston. I loved its feel and its look. I found
that I was able to throw any length of line that is within my ability to throw
without having to think about what I was doing. Its action suited my casting style. But I did not own one.

All rod manufacturers have special deals for working guides, but it was
hard for me to justify buying a Winston, which remained an expensive
proposition even at a discount, especially when I already had so many rods.
Last year at the Fly Tackle Dealer Show, I introduced myself to Tom Morgan
and told him how highly I regard his rods. I also told him that I had not yet
bought one. He explained to me that he was going to do what he could to fur-
ther lower the price to guides so that they could afford to have them, and
then he proceeded to talk about the fishing in his home waters of Montana,
about his love of rivers and trout, and other things that matter. Unlike so
many of the rod manufacturers I spoke with at the show, Tom talked about
fishing, not engineering.

A few months later, a letter arrived at the shop, outlining a new
Winston Rod program for guides. Winstons still weren't cheap, but they
were less expensive than they had been. Tom had been true to his word. He
did what he could to get his rods into the hands of guides. I ordered the
three-piece six-weight and fished it last spring in the heavy water. I fished
it with lead and nymphs. I fished it with long, fine leaders and tiny dries
when I could find rising trout. I took it down the Gunnison River when the
water was fearsome at 6,000 CFS—frothy, pushy, and very difficult to fish.
I cast from a bouncing raft with tons of lead and a stiff abrasion-resistant
leader, banging black Marabou Buggers off the canyon walls and into the
turbulent depths. The Winston was up to the task, and it managed to do
considerably more than just get the job done. It was always a pleasure to
cast. It was crisp, yet smooth—a bit heavier and slower than the Sage five-
weight, but I came to love its accuracy and the joy I always seemed to feel
when I had it in my hand, the beauty I observed when I snugged a favorite

reel into its exquisitely tooled nickel-silver reel seat. No rod will ever give the same measure of joy as a trout, a river, or one's companions, but some rods fit into that world more comfortably than others. Some rods are not just tools, they become something greater. The Winston is a rod you will set aside at the end of the day, lean against a tree, perhaps, in order to go about the business of making a fire and cooking dinner. Every now and then, a green glint will catch your eye as you share stories of the day with your friends, and you'll think, "Damn, what a pretty rod!"

The Winston is my rod of choice during high water on the San Juan. It has the power to lift a long line, a lot of leader, and lead from deep in a heavy run. It easily casts a six-weight line in the hard-blowing winds of spring and, like the Sage five-weight, if I find myself fishing in conditions other than those I expected, it makes the transition. I could not count the number of fish that have taken a midge tied to a 7X leader that was thrown by this six-weight rod. Unlike a good many other six-weights I have fished, its tip is light and supple. It easily absorbs the shock of the strike—even with incredibly fine tippets and tiny hooks. Yet the rod has the muscle to lift and control heavy fish in fast water.

However, this is not the whole story. I am convinced that I could learn to like a great many fine fly rods. Part of the reason I fish this one is because of Tom's kindness, because of his integrity, and because I now own this extraordinary fishing rod because Tom is a man who is true to his word.

Finally, the Powell: Bud has had a Powell Western Sierra for four or five years, and he fishes it everywhere. He says things about it that would make Press Powell cringe—raising expectations way beyond what anyone should expect of a fly rod. He has been known to say that this delicate five-weight is simultaneously the best three- and the best six-weight rod he has ever fished. He regularly loads it with a four-weight line on small streams, and sometimes he even gets around to using the five-weight line recommended by the manufacturer. I have never seen such fanatical devotion to a fly rod in my life.

When we fish small streams together we often take a single rod to pass back and forth, alternating trout or pools. Much of the time the rod we pass back and forth is Bud's Powell. I, too, loved the rod, but I already had several five weights; in fact, I already had several 8½-foot five-weights. There was no way I was going to buy another.

One day last spring, Bud came over to my house in the middle of the afternoon. He had been fishing; I had been writing. We were going to take a break together to cast in a nearby park, but before we walked out the door, he grinned and stuck a shiny green blank in my hand.

"It's the Powell, Steve. You were never going to buy one, and I didn't want you to go through life without it. I know how much you enjoy it."

I built the rod carefully. I matched the deep green wraps and delicate yellow tipping of the factory stick. I glued a black-anodized, up-locking, zebrawood reel seat to the butt. I sanded the corks to fit my hand. Every wrap, every brush loaded with varnish reminded me of Bud's graciousness.

Chop wood, carry water, wrap a fly rod.

Now that it's built, I can't take it out of the tube without a grin. It is not just a fly rod, it's an emblem. It represents a great many profoundly good things, like generosity, kindness, and friendship. I fish this rod because it is the smoothest light rod I own. I like it as a four-weight, and even as a long-line three-weight when casting midges to distant trout. I use it with a five-weight line on small streams. It is a very delicate rod, yet it develops surprising power when you push it hard. However, I think the real reason I fish it is because Bud gave it to me.

This is the rod I imagine under my arm when I imagine myself fishing the streams of old age, not so much because of the way it casts or the way it plays fish, but because I know it will always generate warm memories of rivers, fishing, and friendship.

So you can talk modulus of elasticity, tip deflection, and damping all you want. You can measure resonant frequencies and study the numbers. The fly-fishing press can dig ever deeper into the muck of quantification if it chooses—I guess that's partly what the fly-fishing press is for. In the end, however, we choose fly rods—and the lines that match them, for that matter—by feel, and for reasons that have little to do with numbers.

Find a rod you like. And fish it—a lot.

Beauty is truth, truth beauty.

Old words, but all I need to know.

WATCHING FOR THE WINK

ONE OF MY FAVORITE STRETCHES of water on the San Juan is a remote back channel—a tiny grass-lined runnel barely a foot deep. The surface of the shallow water is often dotted with adult midges. If you look closely, peering through the surface glare with polarized glasses, you can see an enormous variety of submerged insect life drifting with the current. A huge, wary trout has claimed a home here, hugging the bank against the spit of earth that juts into the larger channel where this shallow stream begins. The hook-jawed, five-pound male holds against the bank at the head of the smaller stream. An overhanging willow protects him from eagle and osprey, but the nearby banks are covered only with short grasses and low-lying scrub. Approaching with little cover, a fisherman faces a difficult stalk, a troublesome cast, and a complicated drift before he has any hope of raising and hooking this trout. It is a prime trout, and it occupies a prime lie.

I try for him only when I am alone—partly because I suspect that few fishermen are aware of his presence and I'd like to keep it that way, and partly because this is a fish that requires a commitment of time and patience, a degree of composure, that I find much easier to muster in the absence of company.

On those few occasions when I have been able to hold this trout for a few moments, I have thought that his capture and release are the summation of all that I find good about fishing. The spot where he feeds is as beautiful as any on the river. He is a strong and wary fish. He is near the limit of my angling ability.

If he sees any line or leader denting the surface of the water or casting a shadow, he is gone. If a brightly colored strike indicator floats overhead, he slowly swims upstream to hide beneath a large boulder. Any drag—on line or fly—has the same effect. Any flash of rod or line against the sky, any visible movement above him sends him dashing for cover. When he eats, he holds in shallow water, moving from side to side an inch or two at a time, opening and closing his giant mouth around drifting insects that are caught in currents pushed against the bank at the point of the split.

When I have been able to catch him, I have done so with a long, fine leader, greased to within a few feet of a barely submerged nymph. When I have successfully struck him, it has been because I was able to see his mouth open and close around my fly—not because I have felt a pull, not because I have seen an indicator twitch, not even because I have seen the leader hesitate or behave unnaturally where it entered the water. Only when I have been able to see him take my fly into his mouth have I subsequently felt the jolt of his reaction to my strike, the power of his run for safe haven beneath the upstream boulder. On the few occasions when I have been able to turn him, struggling against his strength, to land and hold him, I have been rewarded with his heft and his trembling in my bare hands, with the stunning sight of his slab-sided body, his shine, his dark green back, and the brilliant red stripe that covers his flanks.

There may be other experiences as good as this in trout fishing, but there are none better. If I had been fishing the way the San Juan is usually fished, I would never have had the experience.

During the summer, and on weekends throughout the year, there are crowds of fishermen on the river. They line up shoulder to shoulder in the

Kittie Pool. They stand in every available piece of water along the shore of the Texas Hole, wading out only as far as the deep, powerful currents will allow, throwing weighted nymphs toward the center of the river. The Upper and Lower Flats are dotted with anglers spread out throughout the shallows. The runs beneath the dam are lined with casters. Boats begin drifting down-river early in the morning, and a constant parade continues to pass until it is nearly dark.

A look at the terminal tackle of the fishermen who congregate in the crowded places, who float by in the drift boats, reveals surprising uniformity. Nearly every rod exhibits the same rig—throughout the day, through every variation of insect. The rig is used when fish lie deep between hatches, feeding on whatever happens to come along, when fish are sipping adults from the surface, and when they are taking nymphs rhythmically in the film. Somewhere on the leader there will be a bright orange indicator made of foam or yarn. A foot or so above the fly, usually placed just above the tippet knot to keep it from sliding down the leader, a split shot or twist of lead is crimped. At the end of the leader there will be a fly or two—perhaps the infamous San Juan Worm in orange or a chamois leach, and below this top fly, a mayfly nymph or midge pupa will dangle.

A single presentation is used with surprising uniformity. Fishermen cast up and across, mend the line as necessary, then watch with their eyes glued to the indicator for signs of a strike.

The technique has become more and more prevalent in the past decade with good reason: it takes fish in difficult water. Fishermen are catching trout in places they could not before, and they are catching them in greater numbers.

The use of this approach is certainly not limited to the San Juan. I have seen it grow until it is, without question, the most commonly used method on much of the better trout water in America.

So what's the problem?

I am not going to make the case that this technique is inferior, morally suspect, or an indication of defective character. Trout-fishing technique is largely a matter of personal preference. What disturbs me about this approach and its widespread use is that a great many new fishermen have not had the opportunity to experience any other method, and the lack of variety in their approach has unnecessarily limited the breadth of their experience. It has also limited their pleasure. Fly fishing should not be a boring, repetitive, redundant routine for catching fish, but an infinitely rich and varied sport.

~

By the time I was learning to fish, the moral superiority of the dry fly had already been long debated, and it was commonly believed then, as it is now, that a fish taken on the dry fly was somehow caught more fairly than one taken on a wet fly. The reasons for this belief were many, but the most compelling argument was made in the language of "chuck and chance." Then, as now, many wet-fly and nymph fishermen searched likely water for trout and waited to feel a tug before setting the hook. This approach seemed arbitrary when compared with the calculated cast made to a visible fish rising to the surface for floating insects.

No one can legitimately question the beauty of seeing a trout rise to a well-drifted fly, the eager anticipation of watching as the fly is taken into a trout's mouth, the sudden thrill of feeling a fish's reaction to the setting of the hook. But there is more, so much more, to fly fishing.

Even in the fifties and sixties, in the days when most wet flies simply searched the water, when the difference between wet- and dry-fly fishing seemed most clear—before we obscured the distinction by fishing "damp" in the film, before there were many who fished hybrid patterns like emergers, cripples, and floating nymphs—there were a few who fished subsurface in a way that made the pejorative label "chuck and chancers" seem ludicrous.

Some truly fine fly fisherman—wet-fly fishermen—played artfully with the leader and with the lead. They greased their gut or monofilament to various lengths in order to control the depth of the fly. They lifted the fly to imitate the behavior of emerging insects. They swam the fly under light tension to imitate swimming nymphs. They stripped streamers, mimicking the darting actions of baitfish. They fished upstream with the rod held high, rapidly retrieving line to maintain contact with the fly. They fished across the stream, dead drift, or pulled the lure away from the bank with quick, short pulls. They fished downstream, dead drift or on the swing, slowing and speeding the fly with careful mends. They struck, not only when they felt a tug, but when they saw a wink—the flash of silver that was a trout moving toward their fly, the brief gleam of white that occurred in the instant when a trout opened and closed its mouth around their imitation.

The best wet-fly and nymph fishermen today continue to use these techniques, and the common denominator is that they rarely wait for a tug, or even for the movement of a strike indicator. The best of them still strike by sight, on the wink.

Nowhere is this more true than in the back channels of the San Juan.

~

During the summer and through the winter, after the reservoir has been drawn down in spring to make room for the water that will rush in during snowmelt, after the river has risen rapidly from the low flows of winter to the torrent of spring releases, after the sudden flooding of the streamside willows, a flooding done with premeditation in order to simulate the natural conditions that existed before the building of the dam—so that the endangered Colorado River pikeminnow might continue to spawn in the lower river—the river settles back to its normal year-round levels and the back channels that had become formidable rivers in their own right at high water become slow, clear, and shallow once again.

The back channels are a wonderful place to fish a dry fly when trout are rising to a hatch of insects. They are unequaled for terrestrial fishing with hoppers, beetles, and crickets cast toward the grassy banks. But, as with most water, the vast majority of food taken there is taken beneath the surface. The wonderful difference is that, rather than lying deep in the water beyond sight, the fish rest within a foot or so of the surface, clearly visible above the rock and gravel bottom, moving from side to side, taking midge larvae and pupae, mayfly nymphs, and aquatic annelids. There is no place I know that is better for sight nymphing, or better for learning to see the wink.

Many fishermen are frustrated on this water. For one thing, the trout are not quite as tame here as they are in some other parts of the river. There are places in the heavily fished water where you can bump a trout with your leg while wading, and it will move a few feet and keep feeding. A poor cast or clumsy wading will send a trout in the back channels running for cover. It is a rare trout in this water that is taken by an angler waiting to feel a tug, or watching to see the indicator move. If you want to take these fish with any regularity, you must wade carefully, cast accurately, and take your eyes off the indicator to watch the fish themselves.

I have another favorite place in the back channels. A place between riffles. A broad flat in a curve of river that is isolated from the crowds by a bit of a hike. Ducks and geese have found this water, too, because they are as fond of crowds as I am. The bufflehead rarely stay close by when I fish there, but it is an unusual morning that does not find me startling a flock on the way in. Cinnamon teal and mergansers come and go on the water, the occasional shoveler works a muddy spot. Canada geese can be found any-where on the river, but in this quiet place they're less edgy, and they often remain in the water nearby when I fish. Willows line the stream on both sides. Across an island of willow, past the deep channel of the main river, the sun illuminates and warms the red and brown sandstone of the south-facing canyon wall. Usually I have this water to myself.

On a popular river it is rare to find such a spot, rarer still to find one that is full of trout. The place is a gem.

Late in the morning, on a typical summer day, rings will appear indi-cating the presence of rising trout. Fish rise in the morning to midges. A well-cast clump or individual adult will take fish throughout the hatch. Later in the day, usually in mid-afternoon, *Baetis* duns will begin to drift through the channel, and the rings will appear again. This is a place where the early summer carpenter ants often appear, sometimes following a particularly heavy rain. Drowned carpenter ants drift through the channel, either as individuals that have been trapped in a torrent or—because they have been caught while mating—as pairs still locked together at the abdomen. Even back-channel trout will rise with abandon to the ants. In August, a cricket or hopper will take fish in this favorite place. But day in, day out, the best way to fish here, and one of the most beautiful, is to sight-nymph between rises to trout feeding beneath the surface in the clear, shallow water.

The only way to catch these trout in the absence of terrestrials, in the absence of a hatch, is with a long cast, a long, fine leader, and a tiny nymph. The only way to strike them is by sight.

I have heard some fly fishers speak disparagingly of this lovely river, lamenting the crowds and the apparent lack of finesse in the technique of so many of the anglers. A few days of watching for the wink on the back channels would cure this impression quickly.

I have taken a few easy fish here. More often I have struggled to see my nymph as it entered the mouth of a wary trout, struggled to cast a low line without commotion, fought to hold a heavy trout with a small hook and fragile leader.

The spring creeks of England are beyond my means—for the most part, so are those of Montana and elsewhere. But this place and this manner of fishing are more than adequate to test my skills, and more than adequate reward for whatever diligence they require.

A RIVER IN DECLINE?

THERE ISN'T AN ANGLER ALIVE who hasn't said at one time or another, "I used to fish the Henry's Fork (the Umpqua, the Bighorn, Lee's Ferry, the Battenkill, the Beaverkill, etc.) but gave it up when the river went to hell." I said that about the San Juan six or seven years ago at a time when the average trout in the river was an eighteen-inch rainbow, and every day you found yourself hooked into some fish that were much larger than that typical trout. Big fish were plentiful—you startled them at every step. It was a time when *Baetis* reliably hatched nearly all year, every afternoon, a time when late summer invariably brought profuse hatches of Pale Morning Duns in the lower water. It was a time when big fish came to the surface to feed on hatched duns and refused to sulk in the depths, preferring nymphs. I said it at a time when the midges were thick on top of the water in the upper river, forming dense black mats of bugs in the eddies that circled round and round with the current in lazy loops, when trout lined up along the current seams taking dozens, perhaps hundreds, of insects with each loud, heart-stopping gulp. It was a time when fishermen routinely asked, "Aren't there any small fish in this river?"

Yet I had decided that the river was in decline.

I made the announcement to Bud one day when we were fishing the Florida, a much smaller river just east of Durango.

"I'm not fishing the Juan anymore," I said. "Too crowded."

I said it to John Flick while mulling over hooks at the fly shop in Durango. I repeated it to anyone who would listen. The litany became so regular, so formalized, that I could chant it without even pausing to think:

The river isn't what it used to be. The fish are thick, but the fishermen are thicker. I am just not going to subject myself to the insanity anymore. How many times can you survive working a good fish for a half hour only to have some buffoon tromp out of the bushes, stomp through the water scaring your fish into the next county, while grinning and shouting a loud "Howdy!"?

How many times can you hike far into the willows, braving armpit-deep sloughs, only to find that your secret place now has five fishermen in it beating the water to death?

How many times can you deal with a lovely hatch and the sight of sipping trout being profoundly disturbed by the yahooing and guffawing of goons yelling to each other at a distance of several hundred yards, "Hey, Bubba, I just hooked another of them monsters on the Day-Glo leech, Wahoooo!"

I've had it. I'm through. You can keep the river; you can keep the big fish; you can keep the crowds. I hate it.

And back then, six or seven years ago, a lot of average fishermen agreed with me. But not the good ones. Not Bud. Not John. I can hear each of them mouthing identical words with the deepest sincerity. "You can't give up on the Juan, Steve. It's too good a river." I didn't give up on her. I found new places away from the crowds. I found chums who were so much pleasure to fish with that the occasional boor or innocently ignorant angler no longer bothered me because I was in the company of friends. I came to focus on my own experience of the river, and the throng receded into the background. But the problem of crowds remains, and it is a situation that anyone who presumes to write about this fishery must address.

Consider the following:

The San Juan is unquestionably the finest fishery in this part of the Rockies. Its reputation is great, and its devotees legion. When an angler arrives to fish it, he is not likely to jump over the hill to another fishery if something goes wrong—if the hatch fails to materialize, if the weather turns sour, if the fish choose to brood and fail to show themselves. It is a destination that, with little exception, remains the first and only choice for many who come to fish it. It often fishes early when few other big-name waters can be fished, and it fishes late—long after brutally cold weather has made trouting a miserable affair up north. In early spring and late fall, in winter, it is one of the rare places in which the multitude of trout-crazed Rocky Mountain anglers can hope to take good fish regularly. And they come. In droves. The good water is three and a half miles long. Three and a half miles. Not a hundred and twenty, like the Deschutes. Not even the thirty or so miles of great fishing on the Bighorn from Yellowtail Dam to Hardin. It doesn't flow through a region that is flush with other well-known water. Three and a half miles to carry all that pressure, all that responsibility. Considering the immensity of the problem, she does pretty well.

And she does horribly.

I am reminded of the oft-paraphrased Dickens: It was the best of rivers. It was the worst of rivers. Or, in the words of Bud Collins, the single most mercurial angler I have ever known, a man who can, on alternate days, even the same day—hell, in the same breath—manage to blurt out, "God what a runaway goddamn screamin', slab-sided fish that was! I love this river, but some asshole keeps fishin' his San Juan Worm just upstream, and when my trout goes through his hole, he tangles me, breaks me off, and then has the gall to turn to me and smile! I hate this place!"

Which about sums it up.

So what to do? Stop writing books about the river? Try to keep it a secret? Too late. The best we can hope for is a little sanity, a little courtesy, some common sense.

I have learned not to go crazy if I hike for a while only to find someone in my private water. There is no private water—not anymore. Instead,

I move on and try new water. I wait for winter to fish the most popular places on the river, and even then I often have to fish elsewhere. If someone moves in on me, I move out. When there is an opportunity, and it looks as if I might be able to speak with an eager neophyte without ruffling feathers, I might deliver a short, friendly soliloquy on etiquette. More often than not, though, I bite my tongue. I take a deep breath. I smile, perhaps a bit sadly, remembering when it wasn't like this, and find another place to fish. The San Juan is a wonderful place to learn about stress management. I know trouting isn't supposed to be like this, but that's the way it often is. There are too many rats.

Years ago a psychologist decided to test a theory regarding population density and aggression by gradually increasing the number of rats living in a confined space. Soon counterproductive, aggressive behavior appeared. Biting, nibbling of tails, unprovoked fights—that sort of thing. Until a given space reaches a certain population density these are rare occurrences, even among rats, but once there are too many rats they become common. We have reached the point of too many rats: in our cities, on our rivers, most everywhere. We're going to have to learn to live with it. The healthy rats, I suspect, will be the ones who manage to slither off into a quiet corner somewhere, not the ones who learn to bite better than the rest, and in that quiet corner we'll do productive things like dream up new bumper stickers (inspired, perhaps, by great oldies like Imagine Whirled Peas, and Subvert the Dominant Paradigm!, or my personal favorite, The Needles Liquor Store: Beer Colder than Your Ex-Wife's Heart).

In the process of trying not to become a better biter, a more competitive and aggressive nibbler, I've discovered some lovely places to fish that I might never have found otherwise. But there are too many rats, no cure in sight, and I can't help missing the river the way it once was.

~

This year some fishermen gave up on the river and the numbers of anglers had nothing to do with their decision. A situation that had been serious because of overcrowding became grave for other reasons. Spring brought heavy runoff, and the river was high. I'd like to think that high water in spring is a natural thing, and we ought to welcome such cycles, but it is not so.

Flows on tailwaters have little to do with natural cycles. If the Bureau of Reclamation were able to operate dams in a vacuum, there would be only one criterion for water release: keep the reservoir filled. But there are other pressures, and they are orchestrated according to the old adage, "The squeaky wheel gets the grease."

The story of water in the West is something of a saga. Once it was told as the noble tale of the greening of arid lands in order to secure prosperity for all. That myth, like its fellow traveler, Manifest Destiny, has been tarnished by history. Some measure of nobility remains in the telling and there were plenty of good intentions. As it is now recited, however, the story of Western water is littered with petty bureaucrats, stupidity, deceit, shortsightedness, and naked greed. The tale has been well and truly told by many fine journalists and historians (Marc Reisner's *Cadillac Desert* and Donald Worster's *Rivers of Empire* are particularly good), but anyone who thinks that the pattern of deception has been broken by the focused light of journalistic truth is naive.

Which is not to say that there is a whole lot we can do now about the management of the San Juan River for trout fishing. The dam project was completed before there was a National Environmental Policy Act—the body of law that requires some consideration of fisheries (and other things) before a dam can be built.

Ripples radiate through all of the water of the West when dam builders consider a new project. The San Juan River is now being affected by one of those new projects, and by its unforeseen ripples.

About fifty miles away, in Durango, the Bureau of Reclamation is planning to build one of its last major water-storage projects. Held up by countless lawsuits filed by those who oppose it, defended by a great many who see it as a much-needed boon to the local economy, the Animas-LaPlata

Project threatens the fishery on the San Juan below Navajo Dam. How? The situation, like almost everything else having to do with Western water, is hopelessly complex, but it boils down to this. Endangered fish (Colorado River pikeminnow, primarily, but also humpback chub and razorback sucker) that live in the San Juan River downstream from its confluence with the Animas River are threatened by the low flows that will occur when water is pumped out of the Animas River into a huge storage reservoir. In an attempt to find a way to mitigate this impact, a multiyear pikeminnow-spawning study has been initiated on the San Juan. The key to the study is increased springtime flows from Navajo Reservoir in order to simulate historic spawning conditions downriver. To keep from emptying Navajo Reservoir, flows at other times of year are being reduced. A fishery that had been relatively stable, a fishery that had grown trout to enormous proportions, a fishery that has had reliable insect hatches for many years, has become unstable, and no one is certain of the consequences.

All this in order to mitigate the impact of a distant project on another river, a project that is ill-conceived and will also threaten the established brown-trout fishery on the Animas River. Environmentalists, conservationists, and anglers are put in the awkward position of appearing to choose between an endangered species and an endangered fishery. All this because we forget how the ripples spread when we tamper with things as complex as rivers, attempting to simulate something we call a natural flow, when we don't have a clue about how complex these things really are. And I say all of this knowing full well that the magnificent fishery that exists on the San Juan did not exist at all before the Bureau of Reclamation built Navajo Dam in the first place. Nothing is simple.

The high flows of spring were created as planned, but along with high flows, there was a level of turbidity that we had not seen before, and it lasted for months. Throughout the spring and into the summer the water was murky. Insects hatched, but the fish did not rise to eat them. The main river was dangerous for wading anglers, and the back channels that were wadable remained turbid. We caught fish, but it was an unpleasant affair. Weighted nymphs and leaders were drifted through the water as much on a prayer as a promise. After months of probing the water for invisible trout, even the most dedicated anglers became bored.

To make matters worse, thousands of small fish were stocked into the river, and for the first time some of the most productive and accessible angling water became home to dozens of gullible, tiny trout. When the flows were finally reduced, the water cleared, but big fish that had eaten beneath the surface throughout the spring continued to do so. Even as a short period of Pale Morning Duns came and went in late July. Even after the *Baetis* reappeared with the shorter days of autumn. The only exception came during the carpenter ant fall, a brief respite from the drudgery of constant nymphing. We could always find a rising fish if we had the patience, but the flats did not light up with rising trout as they once had. The river became a place where a tiny midge pupae (#26 or #28) could take trout anywhere, anytime, but the great variety that had once been the experience of angling on the San Juan had vanished. The typical fish was smaller, and most fishermen would count a number of ten and twelve inchers among their catch on any given day. The joyously incredulous question, "Aren't there any small fish in this river?" was replaced with the joyless lament, "This river isn't what it used to be."

These days, the typical angler remains likely to rave about the fishing. We have grown accustomed to crowds and, after all, this is still a river where most fishermen will hook into a twenty-inch trout or two during a day of fishing; but many of the better anglers are saying that they have given up on the Juan. Guides have begun to speak about moving north, and people who have spent years on the river are beginning to look elsewhere as they plan their future. One week in September, the fishing was actually poor. Not just difficult, not just boring because of a scarcity of rising fish, but downright poor.

Hard fishing with a nymph yielded only a few trout. The river emptied, the crowds dwindled. Guides with the right permits took their clients to the Dolores River, or told them reluctantly that it might be better to postpone their trips.

But nothing is certain—neither plenty, nor famine—and during that week when many had given up hope, I found myself on the river, again in the company of Floyd Ray. I warned him, but he was desperate to fish. A back injury had taken him out of commission for months, and he had done little fishing since winter trips to Chile and New Zealand. The week before he arrived, he had taken his newly healed back to Alaska for ten-pound rainbows easily taken on roe patterns. He returned home wanting to fish the Juan, so we went.

Our morning was okay—a few small fish, a few good fish, all on midge pupae. But the afternoon was unbelievable. In a narrow run pushed hard against an island by a turn in the river, huge trout had collected just prior to the fall spawn. Trout after fresh trout took a pupa, or an egg pattern tied above it on a dropper. None was under nineteen inches. We landed several twenty- to twenty-two-inch trout after long, fast, hard runs. None had a mark on it to indicate a prior encounter with a fisherman. Some of the best fish rose to midges across the current and took a midge emerger drifted in the film with careful, repeated mends. It was, as the happy phrase goes, as good as it gets.

There's a fish story to go with it, a one-that-got-away story, a story I would not believe if I had not been there and no one would believe if anyone other than Floyd were to tell it. It is the story of a trout much bigger than the rest that grabbed a cream-colored egg and ran immediately into the backing, racing downstream. A trout that turned at the riffled water below the run and ran back to our feet. A trout that turned again when he saw us, taking twenty-five feet of line upstream and across, then downstream, again into the backing—ten, twenty, thirty, forty, fifty or more yards into the skinny, white Dacron line without stopping—a trout that repeated this maneuver several times before showing itself on a frantic upstream pass in a single, tumbling, splashing, maw-over-tail leap that buckled our knees. The fish was not just big. It was humongous! Gargantuan! Brobdingnagian!

After many minutes of hanging on for dear life, and many more of trying to nudge the monster toward the net, the fly fell away as the fish began to tire, as Floyd was leading it toward the submerged net. We watched the trout from five feet away as it returned to deep water where we could no longer see it.

"How big do you figure that fish was, Steve?" Floyd asked, the first words he spoke since hooking the trout.

"I don't know, Floyd, but I measured a twenty-seven-inch trout a few months back on the Pine, and your fish was a hell of a lot bigger. I'd guess over thirty inches, and all of ten pounds or more."

"Well, I hate to guess myself, Steve, but he was a hell of a lot heavier than the ten-pounders I landed in Alaska last week."

A river in decline? It's hard to say. Only time will tell. If the crowds continue to grow; if rudeness totally replaces courtesy; if this spring brings a repeat of last year's murk; if small, stocked fish continue to splash in flats that once were filled with heavy, wild, top-feeding sippers; if the big trout continue to sulk near the bottom—I may admit defeat reluctantly. But for now, for me, it remains a place worth fishing.

MENTORS

MUCH OF THE TIME I have spent fishing, I have spent alone. It has always been this way. Even as a child, I spent much of my time alone beside water. Before I was able to fish every day if I chose to—as I did for many summers when I lived near a small mountain stream—even when I lived in the city, even when I had to go to school, even then I spent most days, at least part of the day, playing by a minuscule, polluted, urban trickle named the Third River that ran behind the complex of two-story brick buildings where I grew up. The riparian area beside the river was remarkably intact. Huge, old willows, maples, and oaks grew there, trees that somehow had escaped being cut to make room for houses and factories. The river itself—a small creek, really—trickled over a mud-and sand-silted bottom through one of the most densely populated regions of North America. Somehow minnows survived in the water, and I watched them for hours. Carp swam in those same waters, rising every now and then to eat mosquitoes and crane flies stuck in the surface film.

On the other side of a chain-link fence, a fence intended to keep youthful vandals out, a beautifully maintained golf course straddled the river.

Three arched-stone bridges crossed the stream at intervals of a hundred yards or so. The great complexity of the natural forest had been thinned on the country-club grounds; instead of rising above downed, decaying trees and brush, mature timber shaded manicured grasses. I never realized how powerful the image of those trees, that stream, those stone bridges had been—seen longingly as they were from behind the chain-link fence—until I had grown up and become a serious fisherman. Even now, after having left that place nearly thirty years ago, I remember it in dreams.

My dream is always the same. Somehow I am granted permission to be on the grounds. I am in the river, wading. I move beneath the trees, those huge, old oaks and maples. I wade ever deeper into the wide dream-river. Around me trout are rising. I am carrying a fly rod. I cast to a rising trout, a brown trout, a huge brown trout. It takes the fly, and as it runs away with the hook stuck in the corner of its mouth, I awake.

I have had this dream many times. It is always the same: the river, the trees, the bridges, the brown trout, the wading, the casting, the hooking, the fleeing of the fish. All of these things run deep in me, so deep that they are the stuff of recurring dreams. This river of my youth has merged with the passions of my present and become something more than mere memory.

In my youth I was always by the water alone. In my dreams, I fish it alone. And for much of my adult life I continued to want, mostly, just the company of rivers; rivers and occasionally mentors.

No two of us see things quite the same, no one of us holds all of the truth, and none of us is totally absent understanding.

Temperament is of the past, both the immediate past and a past terribly distant. Temperament is the way we were raised and the way we were born, the accidents of life, and the accidents of far history. Temperament is rooted in immediate yesterdays, and in the very distant yesterdays of the foundations of life itself.

Because we are biological entities.

Because we are the present manifestation of a long line of evolutionary history.

Because we are human.

I spoke of mentors. I spoke of a few wonderful men who took the time to teach me to fish small streams with wet flies. I mentioned some of the many authors whose writing had helped me to understand both the practice and the meaning of fly fishing for trout. Finally I wrote that my greatest mentors had been the rivers themselves, and that none had taught me as much about difficult trout as the San Juan.

This matter of mentorship is an important one to me. Since my father left home many years ago—without warning, without leaving any clues concerning his continued existence—I have been looking for him. I gravitated toward substitutes. I eagerly embraced, and was embraced in return, by teachers who saw in me an eager and willing young person who wanted to absorb and share knowledge and friendship.

One good friend, in a cynical moment, said to me that all successful marriages have as their basis the existence of interlocking neuroses. Although I would be reluctant to paint the picture quite so pathologically, the notion of symbiotic need is not one I reject altogether. I recognize that the origins of my deep affection for my teachers lie in my own sense of loss; but here too, I do not choose to paint a picture of pathology. My great good fortune in finding mentors has, I am certain, been partly due to eagerness and need. But I would not trade the friends, the experiences I have had, for anything. And I have long since stopped being angry that my father left in the way he did.

The anthropomorphism that finds me describing the river as a sentient being probably has its origins in this personal history as well. Yet there is a broader truth in it than simply my own response to loss. Such anthropomorphism is a strong tendency. We all share it, and no amount of deconstructing is sufficient to eradicate its presence.

This is weighty stuff, and not often the overt content of fishing books. But it is there, nonetheless, in virtually all of them. It waits beneath the surface, huge and full of life. It waits to connect with us through mischance or intention every time we go fishing. Many an author has written that we do not go fishing to catch fish, and it is no accident that fishing, instead, so often captures us.

It is not simply a matter of humor to describe angling as an insane passion or a divine malady. It is often both. When fishermen speak of their craving, and wonder aloud just who is catching whom, the involuted meaning of our sport is showing.

Many a truth is spoken in jest.

In matters concerning the environment, we argue with the language and devices of science. We argue the case for pure water and clean air, for undisturbed soil, for the conservation of the purifying power of a forest that is allowed to grow freely. We chart the slow transition of ecosystems. Following cataclysm—fire, avalanche, volcano, earthquake—pioneer species are replaced by other species. In the end, the forest finds what ecologists call climax. Old growth. Richness. Diversity. A forest floor full of decaying matter sustains the life above. The oldest and largest living things—ancient trees, huge underground fungi—live within a time and scale we cannot comprehend. Yet we people this forest with a human understanding. We name the early plants "pioneers." We call the final, ecstatic condition a climax. We designate all of this science, but science, too, is anthropomorphism—even this science of nature we call ecology.

In the field that has come to be known as deep ecology—ecology that requires us to consider the needs and rights of the nonhuman—no epithet is as venomous as this: anthropocentrism. Human-centeredness. Yet how can we escape it?

The extremist would question the validity of all that I have learned from other humans. He would argue that the only legitimate mentor is the earth itself. Jim Bell's gentle wisdom, his searching wet fly, is meaningless to the radical. Bud Collins's mastery of the midge becomes only so much vanity. Haig-Brown is reduced to a pile of meaningless words. Ray Bergman becomes just another member of the hated hooks-and-bullets press. In the vernacular of political correctness, in the heated debate of radical environmentalism, such wisdom is rejected. It is not given directly by the earth, it is given by men, and no matter how wise, no matter how graciously taught or generously shared, the gift is rejected.

Recently I had dinner with a group of friends. It was the birthday of a talented artist, Mary Ellen Long, who lives in the hills above Durango. She now works almost exclusively outdoors. Curators and art historians place her in a category known as earthworks, or site work. Much in the way that the Shinto revere specific places in nature and create shrines in those places to focus attention on their sacredness, Mary Ellen finds things in the woods and she selects them—sometimes simply by photographing them, sometimes by clearing the space around them to make them more evident. Often she carries work done in the woods—paper cast around the trunk of a tree or buried in the ground through a long San Juan Mountains winter—into a gallery. But the woods—her place—is the subject of her work. Many of her friends and colleagues are deeply involved in the very serious issues of conservation and environmentalism. One such colleague whom I had not met before this celebration was present at Mary Ellen's birthday dinner. I was introduced to her by a friend who was seated between us, a poet, who chose to introduce me as a fishing guide and writer of fishing books. I extended my hand in greeting.

Instead of reciprocating with a handshake, she narrowed her eyes, contorted her mouth, and snarled, "I find such behavior execrable!"

The comment took me totally by surprise. In retrospect, I realize that her remarks should not have been totally unexpected. In a world that finds itself moving toward ever more extreme positions, hunting and fishing are rapidly becoming suspect, politically incorrect.

Still, I was shocked. In a single breath, she had repudiated many who had come before me, many whom I love, much that I value, my work, my life.

Our behavior has not always been exemplary, and there is good reason to question the actions of thoughtless fishermen and hunters. Yet my guts tell me she is wrong—emphatically, spectacularly wrong. My guts, influenced as they are by my history, my needs, influenced as they are by my all-too-human experience and emotion, suspect though they may be for any number of reasons, tell me she is wrong. My deepest understanding argues against this radical belief.

The urge to fish is primal. Nothing has connected me with the other as completely. Nothing has connected me with my own human roots, my self, as clearly as the lessons of my angling mentors. I feel as good about the things given to me by these very human humans as I do about the things given to me by the river, and I will not reject them. I will not sacrifice them on the altar of eco-fashion or political correctness.

There is much that is vanity in angling. I choose not to waste my time cataloging it. I will not rail against yuppies, or newcomers, or any number of things so many of us have spent too much time worrying about. I will not bemoan the presence of new BMWs, the dearth of old Chevys, the coming of pesto, or the fact that many a thermos taken to the trout stream now carries espresso instead of coffee. Such criticism is just more of the swagger, the cynicism I lamented earlier.

This is small potatoes.

I indulged my own small-mindedness regarding techno-geeks earlier, and I hope you will forgive me this inconsistency, but as long as I am indulging my foibles, as long as I am bothering to look back at the experience of fishing a river, let me indulge one more need: the need to somehow get a handle on what has transpired.

I rarely fish alone these days. I still find myself in the company of mentors. Often I fish with colleagues and friends. Sometimes I recognize the eagerness, the need, in the eyes of someone who fishes with me. Sometimes I am the mentor.

The earth remains the truest of mentors. The river is of the earth. We are of the earth.

When Jim Bell told me to maintain contact with the fly, he told me what he had learned from the river. When he demonstrated that a gentle word taught more than a loud one, he was behaving in the way that was shown to him by the small streams he preferred to fish. When Ray Bergman laughed at the angler who threw his line over feeding fish, scattering them into deep lies, he laughed like a river, like the fish themselves that scatter. When Bud showed me how to fish a midge, he did so in the way the river had taught him. And when I consider Bud's spirit, I find that his character is much like that of the spate streams he prefers to fish: ambling through quiet times, raging through storms.

The earth remains the truest of mentors. The river is of the earth, and so are we.

My guts tell me that much of the knowledge that has been shared with me by others has come from the river, and I trust it. Many of those I most revere have become wise in the shadow of rivers. My temperament leads me to them for knowledge. The river has been my truest mentor, but there have been others, and I find that the river has often been the mentor of my mentors as well.

I wish that every fisherman—especially those who fish in places as crowded as the San Juan—would come to know the sport in the presence of a wise and gracious teacher. In this regard, I am hopelessly old-fashioned, and I know it. But the problems of contemporary angling require the graciousness and generosity that come with this method of learning, and it is the height of irony to think that now, when we need it more than ever, it has become all too rare an introduction to angling.

What better thing for moderns than the experience of rivers? What worse for the rivers than the onslaught of thoroughly modern men? What will become of our quiet sport when we have peopled our rivers with graceless, competitive anglers?

I had hoped that time would simplify my thoughts, my questions, regarding rivers, that familiarity and time would have clarified my concerns regarding the meaning and purpose of this activity—this sometimes all-consuming activity that is fly fishing for trout—but such is not the case. With the passage of time, my thoughts about rivers and fishing have become more complex, not less. My feelings have merged and mixed with the very water of the river itself and I, no less than my mentors, have begun to resemble the water I choose to fish—places of energy alternately quiet and boisterous, of moods alternately hopeful and despairing, of vision alternately transparent and murky.

Thankfully, these are not often the questions we ask, the thoughts we think, when we fish. It may be true that the unexamined life is not worth living, but it is also true that the overexamined life becomes somewhat tedious. These are the thoughts we sometimes think when we stop fishing, the thoughts we sometimes express when we are asked to by friends who wonder why we do what we do, the thoughts we think when we are confronted with foes who are quick to condemn, quick to snarl, quick to find both our confusion and our passion execrable.

These are the thoughts that come, even before they are fully formed and ready, when we attempt to chronicle the experience of a river.

Winter has come again, though not like the gray winter of years ago, the winter Bud and I searched obsessively for trout and direction, our feet stretching for a ground from which we had somehow floated free; rather, it is a winter of bright, warm days. In mid-January, the deep snows have yet to appear.

The crowds that lingered on the river into the new year have finally dwindled. Although it will probably never again seem like a private place, there is more than enough water for the few who are fishing it. The crowded areas—the Upper and Lower Flats, the catch-and-release water, Lunker Lane, even the Kittie Pool—are sometimes empty. The back channels are a place to go by choice and not necessity. Even now, even after the crowds have gone, I find myself fishing the back channels.

The lake turned over early in January, and for a week or so the water was murky. We searched for trout where we thought they might be, not where we could see them, because we could not see them. We searched with patterns that mimicked the food we found when we screened the water—tiny black and olive midge pupae, slightly larger *Baetis* nymphs in black, gray, and brown—but we had little luck unless we trailed these dull imitations behind gaudy attractors. We cast two-fly rigs of tiny flies that dangled beneath bright annelids and eggs.

Luckily, the river cleared quickly, and now we can see the fish. They lie against the side-slope of the bottom, hugging the walls of deep, narrow channels that wind their way through the willow-lined runs. Late in the morning, the fish rise to hatching midges. This winter the insects seem particularly small.

Months ago, at the height of summer, I went fishing with Slaton White in the mountains north of Durango. We fished a tiny creek in an alpine meadow, a creek that ran into the Animas, a creek whose waters eventually found the San Juan. In this headwater we fished for natives—cutthroat. They were tiny; rarely over ten inches long, often smaller. They were spooky. Lifting the rod to cast might scatter twenty from the middle of a miniature pool—tiny fish would dart like rockets for the safety of the undercut bank. A tangle of scrub—dotted with the yellow of blooming, shrubby cinquefoil, the tarnished white of fading globeflower and marsh marigold—tangled loose line and tore at our ankles. The natives came to small Royal Trudes drifted against the banks. Sometimes we crawled on our knees through the brush. We rarely got the chance for a second cast if the first landed clumsily, or if the line fell over a feeding cutthroat. It was one of my favorite places, and possibly my favorite kind of fishing. But even here, the conversation turned to the San Juan, a river we were connected to by an unbroken ribbon of water seventy-five miles long.

Slaton had never fished in this part of the Rockies before, and he asked me about the various fisheries. When we got around to discussing the San Juan, we spoke, quite naturally, about small flies. It was the tiny midges of winter I had in mind when I said to Slaton that I often fished size #28 flies, but that I'd gladly tie and fish #32s if I could find the hooks.

A few weeks after Slaton's visit, a small package arrived. In it were a gracious letter and a plastic box. Inside the box were the smallest hooks I had ever seen. They were obviously handmade because each was different—their points, eyes, and bends, the forging of the bend into a flat-sided wire, the slight imperfections that existed in every hook, indicated the tap of a hammer, the blow of a chisel, the working of the wire with skilled but very human hands. They were labeled size #32.

I quickly tied a few dry flies and some pupae on the minuscule bronzed hooks.

Those tiny flies were in my box a few days ago when trout were rising to midges in the back channel. I tied one of the dries to an 8X tippet, hoping it might fool a riser. The 8X looked like rope in the tiny eye, but I have had little luck holding fish on the 9X tippet I carry, so I accepted the mismatch and rose to cast. Bufflehead scattered a hundred yards downstream as I stood.

A good-sized trout had moved from the deeper channel near mid-current to eat tiny adult midges that were drifting slowly in the circular currents of a broad, shallow eddy. The fish was eating bugs in no more than eight inches of water, fifty feet upstream from where I stood. He was mere inches beneath the surface. When he rose, his dorsal fin appeared, then his broad back, finally his nose as he grabbed the drifting midges from the surface.

I cast above him, landing only tippet in the current upstream from his snout. I must have cast a dozen times before I finally hooked the fish. His eventual rise to the imitation was slow, and it was all I could do to keep from yanking the fly from his mouth with an eager strike, but I had missed too many fish that way to make the mistake again. As the fish closed his mouth and began to submerge, I lifted quickly. The miniature hook penetrated and held.

The heavy trout turned downstream and ran. My favorite old reel—my best light-leader reel, a worn old Hardy St. George—gave line smoothly. We remained connected for about thirty seconds before the tiny fly, pushed to its limits by the power of the running fish and the opposing inertia of too much line dragging through the water, came free.

Two trout continued to rise against the far bank. I hooked and lost one of them, and finally landed the last, a very lively eighteen incher. I have taken bigger fish from the river. I have fished a lot of small flies. But none pleased me more than that eighteen incher taken on a #32 fly, tied on a handmade hook given to me by Slaton White.

I cannot explain the attraction to small flies. I cannot explain the great joy of fishing such fragile tackle. Partly it is the fact that I know such a thing would have been impossible for me only a few short years ago, before I spent time on this river with people like Bud, and Joe, and Mike. Before I had spent time there by myself. Before the river had worked its way into my body and psyche so thoroughly that I thought of it even when fishing in the mountains.

My memories of the San Juan are abundant. They include the gray days of winter, the high water of spring, the hot, bright afternoons of summer, and the colorful days of fall; big fish that have torn free, others I have held in my hands; mentors, friends; gentle back channels full of difficult, visibly nymphing trout; roaring currents and trout that held deep; wide flats alive with thick fish that took dry flies readily and ran away, taking my breath with them; ducks, geese, eagles, hawks, and heron; mule deer and coyote; mayflies, midges, caddis, stone flies, hoppers, crickets, and ants; the smell of sage brushed by waders while walking to the stream, of ozone lingering after a lightning strike, the fresh scent of a spring morning; the tart taste of apples plucked from the trees of an abandoned orchard and eaten on the banks of the Holy Water; a list too long to compile; a list as rich and full and wonderful as any list can be; a list that only hints at the power of the experience of a river.

A river in danger of being loved to death, for all the right reasons.

CPSIA information can be obtained at www.ICGtesting.com
Printed in the USA
BVOW04s1347140813

328570BV00002B/5/P